OAE 048 Theater

Dahlia B. Arthur

This page is intentionally left blank.

This page is intentionally left blank.

Table of Content

Chapter 1 – Questions 1

Chapter 2 – Answers and Explanations 49

This page is intentionally left blank.

Chapter 1 – Questions

QUESTION 1

How does the genre of "tragicomedy" blend elements of tragedy and comedy in a stage play?

    A.   By having separate tragic and comedic scenes that don't intersect.
    B.   By alternating between moments of intense sorrow and lighthearted humor.
    C.   By avoiding any humorous elements to maintain the seriousness of the tragic aspects.
    D.   By combining tragic events with comic characters to create a unique blend of emotions.

Answer:

QUESTION 2

Which design element primarily refers to the arrangement of objects, actors, and scenery within the performance area?

    A.   Texture
    B.   Repetition
    C.   Space
    D.   Color

Answer:

QUESTION 3

What design principle involves the juxtaposition of different elements to create interest and draw attention?

    A.   Balance
    B.   Emphasis
    C.   Unity
    D.   Contrast

Answer:

QUESTION 4

Which historical period is known for its elaborate and ornate theatrical productions, featuring extravagant costumes and highly stylized performances?

    A.   Renaissance
    B.   Baroque
    C.   Ancient Greece
    D.   Romanticism

Answer:

QUESTION 5

Which theatrical style is known for its use of symbolism, non-linear narrative structures, and exploration of the subconscious mind?

    A.   Realism
    B.   Expressionism
    C.   Neoclassicism
    D.   Absurdism

Answer:

QUESTION 6

What term refers to the process of coordinating and overseeing all aspects of a theatrical production, including budgeting, scheduling, and personnel management?

A. Playwriting
B. Dramaturgy
C. Producing
D. Blocking

Answer:

QUESTION 7

During which stage of production would a theater manager typically work on securing sponsorships, partnerships, and funding for a show?

A. Pre-production
B. Rehearsal
C. Performance
D. Strike

Answer:

QUESTION 8

What is the term for the document that outlines the sequence of scenes, entrances, exits, and movements of actors on stage?

A. Script
B. Blocking
C. Cue sheet
D. Score

Answer:

QUESTION 9

Which theatrical design element primarily focuses on creating the visual appearance of the physical environment where the play takes place?

A. Costume design
B. Set design
C. Lighting design
D. Sound design

Answer:

QUESTION 10

In costume design, what term describes the initial sketches or visual representations of the costumes that designers create during the conceptual phase?

A. Wardrobe plot
B. Rendering
C. Fitting
D. Stitching

Answer:

QUESTION 11

What is the main purpose of lighting design in theater?

    A.   To provide background music
    B.   To enhance the actor's movements
    C.   To create a realistic set design
    D.   To establish mood and atmosphere

Answer:

QUESTION 12

Which ancient Greek playwright is known for his tragic plays like "Oedipus Rex" and "Antigone"?

    A.   William Shakespeare
    B.   Henrik Ibsen
    C.   Euripides
    D.   Sophocles

Answer:

QUESTION 13

Who is often referred to as the "Father of Modern Drama" and wrote plays like "A Doll's House" and "Hedda Gabler"?

    A.   Anton Chekhov
    B.   Bertolt Brecht
    C.   August Strindberg
    D.   Henrik Ibsen

Answer:

QUESTION 14

Which American playwright is known for his works like "Death of a Salesman" and "The Crucible"?

    A.   Tennessee Williams
    B.   Arthur Miller
    C.   Eugene O'Neill
    D.   August Wilson

Answer:

QUESTION 15

What teaching approach focuses on engaging students in learning through hands-on, experiential activities and group collaborations?

    A.   Lecturing
    B.   Directing
    C.   Experiential learning
    D.   Individual study

Answer:

QUESTION 16

When designing theater education programs for children, why is it important to consider age-appropriate material?

- A. To challenge them with complex themes
- B. To expose them to adult content
- C. To ensure safety during performances
- D. To cater to their developmental levels

Answer:

QUESTION 17

What teaching technique involves students taking on roles of characters and improvising scenes to enhance their creativity and understanding of theater concepts?

- A. Monologuing
- B. Analyzing scripts
- C. Role-playing
- D. Memorizing lines

Answer:

QUESTION 18

How does the interdisciplinary nature of theater enrich students' education?

- A. It focuses solely on acting skills
- B. It limits creativity to theatrical contexts
- C. It connects theater with other academic subjects
- D. It emphasizes technical aspects over artistic expression

Answer:

QUESTION 19

In what way does theater promote communication skills beyond the stage?

- A. By encouraging solitary work
- B. By emphasizing memorization
- C. By fostering teamwork and collaboration
- D. By prioritizing technical proficiency

Answer:

QUESTION 20

How does the study of theater contribute to a well-rounded education?

- A. By isolating students from other disciplines
- B. By solely focusing on performance skills
- C. By limiting creativity to scripted content
- D. By promoting critical thinking and empathy

Answer:

QUESTION 21

What is the primary purpose of blocking in theatrical production?

    A.   To determine the script's copyright status
    B.   To design the lighting and sound cues
    C.   To plan and map out the movement and positions of actors on stage
    D.   To create promotional materials for the production

Answer:

QUESTION 22

During the rehearsal process, what is the significance of a "cue-to-cue" rehearsal?

    A.   To finalize the casting decisions
    B.   To rehearse the musical numbers
    C.   To practice the scene changes and technical cues
    D.   To refine the actors' performances

Answer:

QUESTION 23

How does theater contribute to cultural understanding and empathy in society?

    A.   By providing escapism from real-world issues
    B.   By promoting competition among theater companies
    C.   By portraying diverse perspectives and human experiences
    D.   By focusing solely on entertainment value

Answer:

QUESTION 24

How can theater be considered a form of storytelling within the humanities?

    A.   By emphasizing fictional and unrealistic elements
    B.   By exclusively using monologues and soliloquies
    C.   By integrating various artistic elements, such as acting, set design, and music
    D.   By excluding themes related to social issues

Answer:

QUESTION 25

In what ways does theater intersect with historical and cultural contexts in the humanities?

    A.   By focusing solely on contemporary issues
    B.   By excluding references to historical events
    C.   By reflecting the social and political climate of its time
    D.   By disregarding the influence of cultural heritage

Answer:

QUESTION 26

What does the term "ensemble" refer to in theater production?

    A.   The main character in a play
    B.   A solo performance by an actor
    C.   A group of actors working collaboratively as a cohesive unit
    D.   The physical design of the stage set

Answer:

QUESTION 27

What is the significance of theatrical improvisation in actor training?

    A.   It helps actors memorize lines more effectively
    B.   It allows actors to abandon the script entirely
    C.   It enhances spontaneity, creativity, and adaptability on stage
    D.   It ensures actors stay within the boundaries of the director's vision

Answer:

QUESTION 28

In theater, what does the term "blocking" refer to?

    A.   The act of assigning roles and responsibilities to production staff
    B.   The process of mapping out the movement and positions of actors on stage
    C.   The use of visual elements to create a dynamic and visually appealing production
    D.   The strategy for promoting and marketing a theatrical production

Answer:

QUESTION 29

What is the purpose of the exposition in a play's dramatic structure?

    A.   To introduce the main conflict and climax of the play
    B.   To depict the rising action and character development
    C.   To provide background information and context to the audience
    D.   To resolve the conflicts and bring closure to the story

Answer:

QUESTION 30

What distinguishes a well-structured play from one with weak dramatic structure?

    A.   The inclusion of excessive comedic elements
    B.   The complexity of the character's motivations
    C.   The effective organization of plot events and their impact on the audience
    D.   The use of unconventional theatrical techniques

Answer:

QUESTION 31

How does the resolution phase of a play's dramatic structure differ from the climax?

    A.   The resolution phase presents the main conflict, while the climax brings closure to the story.
    B.   The resolution phase is the most intense point of the play, while the climax brings resolution to the main conflict.
    C.   The resolution phase reveals the outcome of the main conflict, while the climax is the turning point of the play.
    D.   The resolution phase involves minor conflicts, while the climax resolves the main conflict.

Answer:

QUESTION 32

What is the purpose of the "subtext" in acting?

    A.   To provide background information about the characters
    B.   To emphasize physical gestures and movements on stage
    C.   To deliver lines with exaggerated emotions
    D.   To convey the underlying thoughts and emotions beneath the dialogue

Answer:

QUESTION 33

What is the significance of active listening in acting?

    A.   To entertain the audience with engaging dialogue delivery
    B.   To synchronize movements and gestures with other actors
    C.   To respond genuinely and spontaneously to fellow actors' lines
    D.   To memorize lines accurately and avoid mistakes

Answer:

QUESTION 34

What does the term "sense memory" refer to in acting techniques?

    A.   The ability to recall lines from memory without hesitation
    B.   The use of imagination to create fictional emotions
    C.   The physical sensations associated with a specific emotional memory
    D.   The precise blocking and movements during a scene

Answer:

QUESTION 35

What is the director's role in shaping the visual elements of a theatrical production?

    A.   To assign specific lines and actions to each actor
    B.   To coordinate the movements of the ensemble during group scenes
    C.   To work with designers to create a unified and cohesive visual concept
    D.   To focus solely on the actors' emotional performances

Answer:

QUESTION 36

What is the primary objective of a director during the rehearsal process?

    A.   To ensure actors memorize their lines perfectly
    B.   To impose their personal artistic vision on the production
    C.   To guide and shape the actors' performances
    D.   To prioritize technical aspects over the actors' performances

Answer:

QUESTION 37

How can a director effectively manage conflicts and creative differences among the production team?

    A.   By dismissing team members with conflicting viewpoints
    B.   By ignoring creative input from the team
    C.   By encouraging open communication and collaborative problem-solving
    D.   By dictating all decisions without considering the team's input

Answer:

QUESTION 38

Who is considered one of the most influential American theater directors, known for his groundbreaking contributions to the concept of "total theater" and immersive experiences?

    A.   Arthur Miller
    B.   Lin-Manuel Miranda
    C.   Robert Wilson
    D.   August Wilson

Answer:

QUESTION 39

Which historical event greatly influenced American theater in the mid-20th century, leading to a surge in socially conscious and politically relevant plays?

    A.   The Civil War
    B.   The Great Depression
    C.   The Industrial Revolution
    D.   The Harlem Renaissance

Answer:

QUESTION 40

Which theatrical form, characterized by colorful masks, elaborate costumes, and stylized movements, originates from Japan?

    A.   Kabuki
    B.   Commedia dell'arte
    C.   Noh
    D.   Peking Opera

Answer:

QUESTION 41

Which theatrical tradition from Africa is characterized by its vibrant drumming, dance, and storytelling performances?

    A.   Butoh
    B.   Haka
    C.   Noh
    D.   Griot

Answer:

QUESTION 42

What is the purpose of obtaining performance licenses and royalties for a theatrical production?

    A.   To pay actors and crew members
    B.   To comply with safety regulations
    C.   To secure the rights to perform a copyrighted work
    D.   To provide insurance coverage for the production

Answer:

QUESTION 43

Which legal document outlines the terms and conditions of an agreement between a theater producer and the creative team, including actors, directors, designers, and crew members?

    A.   Copyright registration
    B.   Liability waiver
    C.   Performance contract
    D.   Safety protocol

Answer:

QUESTION 44

What is the primary function of the "scenery" in a theatrical performance?

    A.   To create a backdrop for the actors' movements
    B.   To provide safety measures for the performers
    C.   To amplify the actors' voices and sound effects
    D.   To control the lighting design on stage

Answer:

QUESTION 45

In a theatrical production, what is the purpose of "blocking" as a stage direction?

    A.   To coordinate the actors' movements with the sound cues
    B.   To direct the audience's attention to specific areas of the stage
    C.   To plan and map out the actors' movements and positions on stage
    D.   To create the desired visual effects with the lighting design

Answer:

QUESTION 46

What is the primary purpose of using makeup in theatrical performances?

    A.   To enhance the actors' natural features for personal satisfaction
    B.   To ensure the actors are recognizable to the audience
    C.   To save time on costume changes during the performance
    D.   To protect the actors' skin from stage lighting

Answer:

QUESTION 47

What is the role of the sound designer in a theatrical production?

    A.   To compose the original music for the play
    B.   To operate the sound equipment during the performance
    C.   To design and coordinate all sound-related elements, including music and effects
    D.   To oversee the actors' vocal training and projection

Answer:

QUESTION 48

Which characterization technique involves creating a detailed background story for a character's life experiences, motivations, and beliefs?

    A.   Monologue
    B.   Physicality
    C.   Backstory
    D.   Blocking

Answer:

QUESTION 49

Which characterization technique focuses on the distinct way a character moves, stands, and uses their body to convey personality?

    A.   Motivation
    B.   Subtext
    C.   Gesture
    D.   Plot

Answer:

QUESTION 50

What is a fundamental principle of improvisation that emphasizes accepting and building upon the ideas presented by fellow actors?

    A.   Denial
    B.   Blocking
    C.   Yes, And...
    D.   Contradiction

Answer:

QUESTION 51

Which improvisation technique involves developing a scene without the use of spoken language, relying solely on physical actions and gestures?

    A.   Mime
    B.   Monologue
    C.   Soliloquy
    D.   Exposition

Answer:

QUESTION 52

Which dramatic genre is characterized by its focus on the everyday lives of ordinary people, often portraying their struggles and challenges with realism and empathy?

    A.   Tragedy
    B.   Comedy
    C.   Melodrama
    D.   Realism

Answer:

QUESTION 53

What major theme in drama explores the internal conflicts and moral dilemmas faced by individuals as they make difficult choices between right and wrong?

    A.   Identity
    B.   Love
    C.   Conflict
    D.   Morality

Answer:

QUESTION 54

Which historical period of drama emphasized emotional intensity, irrational behavior, and the exploration of the human psyche, often featuring tragic protagonists facing inevitable downfall?

    A.   Renaissance
    B.   Classical
    C.   Romanticism
    D.   Modernism

Answer:

QUESTION 55

Which teaching approach in drama encourages students to explore and interpret characters and scenes through their personal experiences and emotions?

    A.   Experiential learning
    B.   Direct instruction
    C.   Behaviorism
    D.   Lecture-based

Answer:

QUESTION 56

What teaching method involves students working collaboratively to create and perform original theatrical pieces based on a specific theme or concept?

- A. Lecture-based
- B. Script analysis
- C. Devising
- D. Behaviorism

Answer:

QUESTION 57

Which teaching technique encourages students to analyze and critique performances by applying established criteria, enhancing their ability to assess theatrical works objectively?

- A. Reflective journaling
- B. Improvisation
- C. Project-based learning
- D. Performance evaluation rubrics

Answer:

QUESTION 58

During which stage of artistic development are children most likely to engage in imaginative play, make-believe scenarios, and simple role-playing activities?

- A. Pre-operational stage
- B. Concrete operational stage
- C. Formal operational stage
- D. Post-operational stage

Answer:

QUESTION 59

What is a key benefit of drama activities for adolescents in terms of their social and emotional development?

- A. Enhancing abstract reasoning
- B. Reinforcing concrete thinking
- C. Fostering empathy and emotional intelligence
- D. Encouraging conformity

Answer:

QUESTION 60

Which concept refers to the idea that adolescents in drama/theater develop a stronger sense of self-identity and self-expression through exploring various roles and characters?

- A. Egocentrism
- B. Identity crisis
- C. Role confusion
- D. Self-actualization

Answer:

QUESTION 61

When selecting a play for a high school production, which factor should a theater teacher prioritize to ensure it resonates with the target audience and aligns with the educational goals?

A. The personal preference of the director
B. A popular play from the previous year
C. Relevance to students' lives and experiences
D. The availability of elaborate set designs

Answer:

QUESTION 62

When considering the technical aspects of a play, which consideration is crucial in selecting a production that can be successfully executed within the available resources?

A. Complex lighting effects
B. Multiple intricate set changes
C. Elaborate costume designs
D. Lengthy monologues

Answer:

QUESTION 63

Which dramatic form emphasizes exaggerated characters and intense emotions, often featuring a clear distinction between heroic protagonists and villainous antagonists?

A. Tragedy
B. Melodrama
C. Absurdist drama
D. Comedy

Answer:

QUESTION 64

In which dramatic form are everyday situations and conversations depicted in a realistic and often humorous manner, highlighting the absurdities of human behavior?

A. Farce
B. Tragedy
C. Satire
D. Epic theater

Answer:

QUESTION 65

In the context of theater, how can cultural factors influence the portrayal of characters and themes in a play?

A. By determining the ticket prices and theater's financial success.
B. By shaping the costumes, set designs, and language used by the characters.
C. By dictating the actor's performance style and directing choices.
D. By influencing the availability of funding for theater productions.

Answer:

QUESTION 66

How does the political climate of a region impact the themes and narratives explored in theater during that time?

A. It has no effect on theater; theater remains an apolitical art form.
B. It can lead to the censorship of certain plays or themes considered politically sensitive.
C. It encourages theater practitioners to avoid controversial topics entirely.
D. It fosters a spirit of rebellion, leading to an increase in experimental and avant-garde theater.

Answer:

QUESTION 67

How can economic factors influence the accessibility and availability of theater to different social classes?

A. By prioritizing blockbuster productions that cater to a mass audience.
B. By implementing strict dress codes that exclude certain social classes.
C. By offering discounts and subsidies to low-income individuals and students.
D. By staging plays that only resonate with a specific social or economic group.

Answer:

QUESTION 68

How does Greek classical theater differ from modern theater in terms of the role of the chorus?

A. In modern theater, the chorus is absent, while Greek classical theater heavily relies on it.
B. In both Greek and modern theater, the chorus serves a purely decorative purpose.
C. In modern theater, the chorus is primarily responsible for delivering the protagonist's lines.
D. In both Greek and modern theater, the chorus represents the main antagonist.

Answer:

QUESTION 69

How does the concept of "verisimilitude" in Renaissance theater influence the portrayal of characters and settings?

A. It prioritizes historically accurate representation over emotional depth in characters.
B. It requires characters to speak in verse and rhyme, limiting their natural expression.
C. It encourages the use of minimalistic sets to focus on character development.
D. It aims to create a semblance of reality while allowing artistic liberties in characters and settings.

Answer:

QUESTION 70

How did the "Theatre of the Absurd" movement challenge traditional theatrical conventions?

A. By promoting sentimentalism and emotional catharsis in its plays.
B. By adhering strictly to the classical three-act structure in all productions.
C. By emphasizing logical and straightforward narratives in its plays.
D. By presenting a fragmented, illogical, and surreal depiction of the human condition.

Answer:

QUESTION 71

What themes were commonly explored by Anton Chekhov in his plays?

 A. Themes of hope, optimism, and idealism in human relationships.
 B. Themes of social justice and the struggle of the working class.
 C. Themes of existentialism, the passing of time, and the search for meaning.
 D. Themes of romantic love and the triumph of good over evil.

Answer:

QUESTION 72

Which of Molière's plays is a satirical critique of religious hypocrisy and fanaticism?

 A. "Tartuffe"
 B. "The Misanthrope"
 C. "The School for Wives"
 D. "The Imaginary Invalid"

Answer:

QUESTION 73

How does Caryl Churchill's play "Top Girls" challenge traditional theatrical storytelling techniques?

 A. By using a linear and chronological narrative structure.
 B. By employing a single protagonist with clear motivations and goals.
 C. By intertwining multiple historical periods and perspectives.
 D. By adhering strictly to the Aristotelian unities of time, place, and action.

Answer:

QUESTION 74

What was a significant innovation introduced by Bertolt Brecht in his theatrical productions?

 A. Elaborate and ornate set designs to create a sense of realism.
 B. The concept of "alienation" to remind the audience they are watching a play.
 C. The use of improvisation and audience participation in every performance.
 D. Strict adherence to the traditional Aristotelian dramatic structure.

Answer:

QUESTION 75

Which significant development in theatrical production during the Renaissance era allowed for more elaborate and complex stage designs?

 A. Introduction of electric lighting to create various lighting effects.
 B. Adoption of movable sets and wagons that could be easily changed during performances.
 C. Use of microphones and sound systems for amplified sound.
 D. Incorporation of live animals in performances to add realism.

Answer:

QUESTION 76

How did the emergence of "Theatre of Cruelty," as conceived by Antonin Artaud, impact European theatrical performance?

- A. It focused on producing light-hearted comedies to entertain the masses.
- B. It advocated for strict adherence to traditional dramatic conventions.
- C. It sought to evoke primal emotions and challenge conventional perceptions of reality.
- D. It encouraged the use of elaborate and intricate costumes and props.

Answer:

QUESTION 77

Which theme is commonly explored in the works of Irish playwrights such as Sean O'Casey and Brian Friel?

- A. Themes of aristocracy and social class hierarchy.
- B. Themes of revolutionary nationalism and political upheaval.
- C. Themes of romantic love and courtship.
- D. Themes of family dysfunction and interpersonal conflicts.

Answer:

QUESTION 78

What theatrical style was popularized by Henrik Ibsen in the late 19th century, particularly in his play "A Doll's House"?

- A. Expressionism
- B. Realism
- C. Surrealism
- D. Absurdism

Answer:

QUESTION 79

Which theatrical movement was heavily influenced by Sigmund Freud's theories on the subconscious mind and dreams?

- A. Romanticism
- B. Symbolism
- C. Expressionism
- D. Surrealism

Answer:

QUESTION 80

When adapting a classic novel into a stage play, what is a crucial consideration for maintaining the essence of the original work?

- A. Reducing the number of characters and subplots to streamline the narrative.
- B. Modernizing the language and setting to make it more relatable to contemporary audiences.
- C. Staying true to the core themes and character motivations while making necessary adjustments for theatricality.
- D. Incorporating multimedia elements to enhance visual appeal.

Answer:

QUESTION 81

What writing technique can enhance the development of complex characters in a stage play?

- A. Limiting characters' dialogue to essential plot points only.
- B. Using monologues to reveal characters' inner thoughts and emotions.
- C. Minimizing conflicts between characters to avoid complexity.
- D. Avoiding subtext and ambiguity in characters' actions and motivations.

Answer:

QUESTION 82

Why is understanding dramatic structure crucial in the process of playwriting?

- A. It helps ensure that the play's setting is historically accurate.
- B. It ensures that the play includes a diverse cast of characters.
- C. It provides a framework for organizing the plot and its emotional journey.
- D. It guarantees a specific genre or style for the play.

Answer:

QUESTION 83

How can the technique of improvisation be utilized in generating ideas for a stage play?

- A. By scripting every detail of the play beforehand to prevent deviation from the planned narrative.
- B. By encouraging actors to spontaneously create scenes and dialogue during rehearsals.
- C. By using elaborate set designs to inspire the storyline and character development.
- D. By restricting the actors to predetermined character archetypes during improvisation.

Answer:

QUESTION 84

Which method of research and information gathering can be particularly useful when writing a historical period play?

- A. Conducting interviews with contemporary experts on the subject matter.
- B. Using fictional sources to imagine how people might have lived during that period.
- C. Relying solely on secondary sources like books and articles.
- D. Refraining from any research to avoid potential inaccuracies.

Answer:

QUESTION 85

How can the technique of playmaking facilitate collaborative idea generation in theater?

- A. By strictly assigning individual tasks to each collaborator to avoid overlap.
- B. By encouraging group discussions and brainstorming sessions to explore ideas collectively.
- C. By limiting creative input to only a few key members of the team.
- D. By avoiding feedback and critique to maintain artistic independence.

Answer:

QUESTION 86

How does the setting of a play contribute to the communication of ideas and emotions?

    A.   It dictates the actors' movements and blocking on stage.
    B.   It establishes the historical context of the play's events.
    C.   It provides a backdrop that enhances the mood and atmosphere of the play.
    D.   It determines the order of scenes in the script.

Answer:

QUESTION 87

What role does the theme of a play play in structuring the script?

    A.   It influences the choice of actors for specific roles.
    B.   It determines the sequence of events in the play.
    C.   It provides the underlying message and purpose of the entire script.
    D.   It sets the tone for the stage design and lighting.

Answer:

QUESTION 88

In structuring a script, how can the use of foreshadowing be effective in engaging the audience?

    A.   By revealing all major plot twists and resolutions early in the play.
    B.   By using symbolism and metaphors that confuse the audience.
    C.   By hinting at future events and creating anticipation for what will unfold.
    D.   By employing an unreliable narrator to confuse the audience.

Answer:

QUESTION 89

What is the most critical aspect of effective communication within a theatrical production team?

    A.   Setting strict deadlines for tasks
    B.   Assigning specific roles and responsibilities
    C.   Establishing open and respectful channels of communication
    D.   Providing constant feedback and criticism

Answer:

QUESTION 90

How can theater teachers encourage a sense of community involvement in a school production?

    A.   By strictly limiting parent involvement to avoid conflicts
    B.   By organizing exclusive cast events separate from the school community
    C.   By actively engaging parents, teachers, and students in various production aspects
    D.   By avoiding any interaction with the school's administration

Answer:

QUESTION 91

Which theater professional is primarily responsible for coordinating and overseeing the technical and artistic aspects of a production?

   A.   Producer
   B.   Stage Manager
   C.   Technical Director
   D.   Costume Designer

Answer:

QUESTION 92

What is the primary role of a theatrical producer in a production?

   A.   Designing and executing the lighting plan
   B.   Creating the promotional materials for the show
   C.   Managing the financial and business aspects of the production
   D.   Directing and guiding the actors during rehearsals

Answer:

QUESTION 93

When selecting a play for a high school production, what is a key factor that theater teachers should consider?

   A.   The popularity of the play among professional theaters
   B.   The number of musical numbers in the play
   C.   The age-appropriateness of the content for the student actors and audience
   D.   The availability of famous actors for casting

Answer:

QUESTION 94

What is a significant consideration when selecting a play for a community theater with limited financial resources?

   A.   The availability of elaborate set and costume designs
   B.   The length of the play, favoring shorter productions
   C.   The availability of expensive and complex technical effects
   D.   The royalty fees and overall production costs

Answer:

QUESTION 95

What is the purpose of obtaining performance rights or licenses for a play?

   A.   To ensure the play is historically accurate
   B.   To guarantee exclusive rights to the play's script
   C.   To protect against copyright infringement and legal disputes
   D.   To receive discounts on production costs

Answer:

QUESTION 96

Why is it essential for theater producers to have liability insurance for their productions?

- A. To cover the costs of hiring professional actors
- B. To ensure that the play is well-received by the audience
- C. To protect against potential accidents, injuries, or property damage during the production
- D. To guarantee financial profits from the production

Answer:

QUESTION 97

What is an effective approach for theater teachers to assess the artistic abilities of potential actors during auditions?

- A. Asking them to perform a monologue
- B. Assigning complex choreography routines
- C. Evaluating their academic qualifications in theater arts
- D. Requesting a detailed written analysis of a play

Answer:

QUESTION 98

What is the primary consideration when selecting a technical director for a theatrical production?

- A. Their proficiency in performing on-stage technical roles
- B. Their experience and knowledge in technical aspects of theater
- C. Their popularity and social media following
- D. Their ability to design costumes and sets

Answer:

QUESTION 99

Why is it important for theater producers to create a detailed production schedule?

- A. To ensure the actors have enough time for rehearsals
- B. To prevent the production from going over budget
- C. To ensure the production runs on time and smoothly
- D. To allocate specific roles to the production staff

Answer:

QUESTION 100

What is a primary consideration when budgeting for a theatrical production?

- A. Allocating the majority of the budget for costumes and props
- B. Ensuring a luxurious venue for the performances
- C. Keeping production costs within financial constraints
- D. Focusing on elaborate marketing campaigns

Answer:

QUESTION 101

Which dramatic style is characterized by the use of exaggerated and stylized movements and gestures?

- A. Naturalism
- B. Realism
- C. Expressionism
- D. Absurdism

Answer:

QUESTION 102

In which genre would you most likely find elements of mystery, suspense, and unexpected plot twists?

- A. Comedy
- B. Tragedy
- C. Farce
- D. Thriller

Answer:

QUESTION 103

Which dramatic movement challenged traditional norms and sought to represent the inner workings of the human mind, often using symbolism and non-linear narratives?

- A. Realism
- B. Naturalism
- C. Expressionism
- D. Absurdism

Answer:

QUESTION 104

What major theme in drama explores the consequences of excessive ambition and hubris, leading to the downfall of a once-respected character?

- A. Love and sacrifice
- B. Fate and destiny
- C. Loyalty and betrayal
- D. Tragic flaw and pride

Answer:

QUESTION 105

When evaluating acting skills in elementary school students, which criterion should be emphasized to encourage their growth and development?

- A. Complex character motivations
- B. Utilization of advanced vocal techniques
- C. Consistent memorization of lines
- D. Expressive physical gestures and body language

Answer:

QUESTION 106

What should a theater teacher consider when evaluating the technical aspects of a middle school production, such as set design and props?

A. The incorporation of advanced lighting techniques
B. The adherence to historically accurate details
C. The complexity of Shakespearean language
D. The safety and functionality of the set and props

Answer:

QUESTION 107

Which principle of acting emphasizes the need for actors to fully understand the motivations, emotions, and background of their characters?

A. Breaking the fourth wall
B. Emotional recall
C. Stanislavski's "Magic If"
D. Blocking and stage movement

Answer:

QUESTION 108

During an acting class, a student asks about the significance of improvisation in developing acting skills. How would you explain the benefits of improvisational exercises to enhance acting abilities?

A. Disregard improvisation as it has no relevance in acting.
B. Explain that improvisation is solely for comedic performances.
C. Discuss how improvisation enhances spontaneity, creativity, and adaptability.
D. Suggest that improvisation is a distraction from scripted acting.

Answer:

QUESTION 109

You are directing a school play and have received audition videos from prospective actors. One actor has a strong stage presence and delivers lines with confidence, but struggles with portraying emotional depth. Another actor displays remarkable emotional range but is less confident in their delivery. How would you approach casting these actors in roles that require both confidence and emotional depth?

A. Cast the confident actor for roles requiring emotional depth and coach them.
B. Cast the emotionally expressive actor for all roles and work on their confidence.
C. Cast both actors in roles that emphasize their respective strengths.
D. Choose neither actor and seek someone who excels in both areas.

Answer:

QUESTION 110

During auditions, you notice that one actor has excellent chemistry with another actor who is auditioning for a different role. How might you utilize this chemistry to make casting decisions?

A. Cast both actors in their respective roles to maintain the chemistry.
B. Cast the actor with chemistry in the role that aligns with their strengths.
C. Disregard the chemistry as it may not translate to the final production.
D. Cast the actors together in a completely different set of roles.

Answer:

QUESTION 111

As a theater teacher, you are guiding students in designing the set for a play set in two contrasting locations: a cozy cottage and a bustling city street. How would you encourage the students to effectively convey these contrasting settings through set design?

- A. Use the same set elements for both locations to simplify the design.
- B. Focus solely on intricate details to differentiate the settings.
- C. Incorporate distinct visual elements and props for each location.
- D. Avoid visual differences to maintain a consistent design style.

Answer:

QUESTION 112

When designing costumes for a historical play set in the Victorian era, a student proposes using modern fabrics to create a more comfortable and practical wardrobe for the actors. How would you guide the student in making a decision that balances historical accuracy and practicality?

- A. Prioritize modern fabrics for comfort and ease of movement.
- B. Use exclusively historically accurate fabrics, regardless of comfort.
- C. Combine historically accurate silhouettes with modern fabrics for a compromise.
- D. Discard historical accuracy to prioritize modern practicality.

Answer:

QUESTION 113

You are teaching a script analysis workshop, and a student asks why understanding the cultural context of a play is important for interpretation. How would you explain the significance of cultural context in script analysis?

- A. Emphasize that cultural context has no impact on script interpretation.
- B. Explain that cultural context only affects historical plays, not contemporary ones.
- C. Discuss how cultural context shapes characters, themes, and societal dynamics.
- D. Suggest that cultural context is irrelevant if the play is set in a fictional world.

Answer:

QUESTION 114

While analyzing a script, you notice that the dialogue includes metaphorical language and symbolism. How might you guide actors in effectively conveying these symbolic elements during their performances?

- A. Advise actors to focus solely on delivering their lines with clarity.
- B. Instruct actors to downplay symbolic elements to avoid confusion.
- C. Encourage actors to explore the metaphorical meanings behind the dialogue.
- D. Recommend that actors ignore symbolic elements to prioritize emotional expression.

Answer:

QUESTION 115

In a high school theater class studying American playwrights, the teacher decides to focus on the works of Arthur Miller. To engage the students, the teacher plans to present a short scene from one of Miller's plays and then asks the students to guess the play's title. The selected scene involves a family dinner where a father struggles to conceal a dark secret from his sons. Which play by Arthur Miller is the teacher most likely showcasing?

- A. "Death of a Salesman"
- B. "A View from the Bridge"
- C. "All My Sons"
- D. "The Crucible"

Answer:

QUESTION 116

A theater teacher is introducing the concept of method acting to their college students. To demonstrate the impact of method acting on American theatrical performance, the teacher shares a brief biography of an influential actor who significantly contributed to its development. This actor was known for immersing himself deeply into his characters and famously played Stanley Kowalski in "A Streetcar Named Desire" on Broadway. Who is this prominent actor?

- A. Marlon Brando
- B. James Dean
- C. Laurence Olivier
- D. Humphrey Bogart

Answer:

QUESTION 117

A high school drama teacher is exploring contemporary American drama with their students. They decide to stage a play that addresses the complexities of family relationships and communication in the digital age. The chosen play revolves around a family's struggle to reconnect after the parents' divorce, and how technology affects their interactions. Which play is the drama teacher likely to select for this exploration?

- A. "August: Osage County" by Tracy Letts
- B. "The Flick" by Annie Baker
- C. "Clybourne Park" by Bruce Norris
- D. "Next to Normal" by Tom Kitt and Brian Yorkey

Answer:

QUESTION 118

A theater instructor is preparing a lesson on traditional Asian theater forms and wants to emphasize the use of stylized movements and masks in one particular form. This theater tradition originated in Japan and often features historical or supernatural themes. What theater form is the instructor likely to focus on during the lesson?

- A. Noh
- B. Kabuki
- C. Beijing Opera (Peking Opera)
- D. Wayang Kulit

Answer:

QUESTION 119

In a university theater course that explores the works of prominent playwrights, the professor assigns a play that examines the psychological impact of apartheid in South Africa. The play centers around a black township family and their struggle for freedom and equality. Which playwright and play is the professor most likely to have assigned?

- A. Athol Fugard - "Master Harold and the Boys"
- B. Augusto Boal - "Theatre of the Oppressed"
- C. Wole Soyinka - "Death and the King's Horseman"
- D. Griselda Gambaro - "Information for Foreigners"

Answer:

QUESTION 120

A theater teacher is discussing the contributions of a renowned lighting designer who revolutionized stage lighting in the 20th century. This designer is known for using light as an integral part of storytelling and creating visually stunning stage productions. Who is this prominent lighting designer?

    A.   Jo Mielziner
    B.   Robert Edmond Jones
    C.   Jennifer Tipton
    D.   Jules Fisher

Answer:

QUESTION 121

A drama teacher is designing a workshop focused on absurdism, a theatrical movement known for its exploration of the human condition through irrational and nonsensical situations. During the workshop, the students will engage in various improvisational exercises to grasp the essence of absurd theater. Which influential playwright is most closely associated with the genre of absurdism?

    A.   Samuel Beckett
    B.   Anton Chekhov
    C.   Henrik Ibsen
    D.   Tennessee Williams

Answer:

QUESTION 122

A drama teacher is planning a lesson to introduce Stanislavski's method of acting to their students. To demonstrate the key principles, the teacher decides to have the students participate in an exercise where they delve into their characters' emotional memories and use them to inform their performances. Which term is often used to describe this Stanislavski technique?

    A.   Emotional recall
    B.   Physical theater
    C.   Dialect coaching
    D.   Viewpoints

Answer:

QUESTION 123

An elementary school drama teacher is planning a theater program to encourage creative expression and build confidence in young students. The teacher wants to select a play that features a diverse range of characters and provides opportunities for every student to have a significant role. Which popular children's play is the teacher likely to choose?

    A.   "The Little Mermaid" by Hans Christian Andersen
    B.   "Alice in Wonderland" by Lewis Carroll
    C.   "Peter Pan" by J.M. Barrie
    D.   "The Lion, the Witch, and the Wardrobe" by C.S. Lewis

Answer:

QUESTION 124

During a theater workshop on improvisation, the instructor divides the students into pairs and asks them to create a short scene without any prior discussion or planning. One pair starts their scene by miming the action of cooking in a kitchen, while the other pair begins with a conversation between two friends in a park. After a few minutes, the instructor asks the pairs to switch locations and continue their scenes. What improvisational technique is the instructor encouraging the students to explore?

- A. Environment Swap
- B. Character Swap
- C. Time Warp
- D. Genre Shift

Answer:

QUESTION 125

A theater teacher is conducting an advanced improvisation class and wants to challenge the students to create complex and emotionally engaging scenes. The teacher instructs the students to perform a series of scenes that explore different emotional states without using any words. The students are only allowed to use physical gestures and facial expressions to convey their emotions. What improvisational technique is the teacher emphasizing in this exercise?

- A. Mime
- B. Pantomime
- C. Physical Theatre
- D. Tableau

Answer:

QUESTION 126

As a theater director prepares for a new production, they decide to hold auditions to select the cast members. During the audition process, the director notices that one actor's performance stands out due to their strong emotional connection to the character and convincing portrayal. However, the actor lacks experience and may need more guidance during rehearsals. What role of the director is highlighted in this situation?

- A. Casting Director
- B. Acting Coach
- C. Dramaturg
- D. Set Designer

Answer:

QUESTION 127

In the process of directing a classic play for a community theater production, the director faces a challenge in updating certain elements of the script to make it more relevant to modern audiences while still honoring the original story's essence. The director wants to maintain the play's authenticity while incorporating subtle changes. What role of the director is most evident in this situation?

- A. Playwright
- B. Dramaturg
- C. Translator
- D. Conceptualizer

Answer:

QUESTION 128

A high school theater teacher is planning the school's next production and wants to choose a play that explores relevant social issues while also providing substantial roles for a diverse cast of students. The teacher seeks a thought-provoking script that sparks discussions about identity, prejudice, and acceptance. Which play is the theater teacher most likely to select?

    A. "Romeo and Juliet" by William Shakespeare
    B. "To Kill a Mockingbird" by Harper Lee (adapted for the stage)
    C. "Our Town" by Thornton Wilder
    D. "The Importance of Being Earnest" by Oscar Wilde

Answer:

QUESTION 129

A college theater professor wants to challenge their advanced students with a play that combines elements of surrealism, symbolism, and nonlinear storytelling. The professor is seeking a script that encourages innovative staging and creative interpretations. Which play is the theater professor most likely to choose for this experimental production?

    A. "A Midsummer Night's Dream" by William Shakespeare
    B. "Waiting for Godot" by Samuel Beckett
    C. "The Glass Menagerie" by Tennessee Williams
    D. "The Crucible" by Arthur Miller

Answer:

QUESTION 130

When selecting a play for a theatrical production, which factor should be given the highest priority?

    A. Popularity and familiarity with the audience.
    B. Availability and affordability of performance rights.
    C. Alignment with the theater company's artistic vision and mission.
    D. The complexity of the technical elements required for the production.

Answer:

QUESTION 131

When considering age-appropriateness for a play's content, which approach should a theater teacher take?

    A. Choose a play with mature themes to challenge and educate the students.
    B. Avoid any controversial themes to ensure the play's broad appeal.
    C. Prioritize plays with light-hearted, comedic content to keep the audience entertained.
    D. Carefully assess the play's themes and content to match the maturity level of the intended audience.

Answer:

QUESTION 132

Which legal document is essential for securing the rights to produce a copyrighted play?

    A. Liability release form.
    B. Memorandum of Understanding (MOU) with the playwright.
    C. Performance contract with the venue.
    D. Trademark registration for the play's title.

Answer:

QUESTION 133

What legal concept helps protect a theater producer from personal financial responsibility in case of unforeseen accidents during a production?

    A. Intellectual property rights.
    B. Limited liability protection.
    C. Contractual indemnification.
    D. Occupational Safety and Health Administration (OSHA) compliance.

Answer:

QUESTION 134

When selecting artistic staff, which quality should be the highest priority for a theater teacher?

    A. Years of experience in the theater industry.
    B. Familiarity with the specific play being produced.
    C. Ability to work within a tight budget.
    D. Creativity and a strong artistic vision.

Answer:

QUESTION 135

What is the primary purpose of holding auditions for a theatrical production?

    A. To select the most experienced actors for the roles.
    B. To provide an opportunity for actors to showcase their talents.
    C. To test the actors' ability to memorize lines quickly.
    D. To evaluate the actors' chemistry with the production team.

Answer:

QUESTION 136

A theater teacher has been assigned to manage a school play with a limited budget. How should the teacher prioritize expenses to ensure a successful production?

    A. Allocate the majority of the budget to costumes and set design for a visually appealing show.
    B. Invest in high-tech lighting and sound equipment for a memorable theatrical experience.
    C. Allocate funds primarily to marketing and promotion to attract a larger audience.
    D. Prioritize essential production elements like script rights and safety measures, then distribute the remaining funds accordingly.

Answer:

QUESTION 137

A theater teacher is planning a theatrical production and needs to create a comprehensive schedule. What is the best approach for handling unexpected delays during rehearsals?

    A. Extend rehearsal hours to make up for lost time and ensure the production stays on track.
    B. Reduce the number of technical rehearsals to allow for additional time for rehearsals with the cast.
    C. Build buffer time into the schedule to account for potential delays and keep the production on schedule.
    D. Cancel non-essential rehearsals to allow the cast and crew more time to prepare for the performance.

Answer:

QUESTION 138

When designing the set for a tragic play, which design principle should the theater teacher focus on to evoke the appropriate emotions in the audience?

    A.   Unity and coherence in the set design.
    B.   Bright and contrasting colors to create a visually striking stage.
    C.   Use of abstract and non-representational shapes to challenge the audience's perception.
    D.   Emphasis on symmetry and repetition to create a sense of stability and balance.

Answer:

QUESTION 139

When selecting costumes for a historical theater production, which factor should the theater teacher prioritize?

    A.   Ensuring the costumes accurately represent the fashion of the historical period.
    B.   Choosing modern, comfortable fabrics to ensure the actors' ease of movement.
    C.   Prioritizing elaborate and ornate costumes to impress the audience visually.
    D.   Selecting costumes that match the personal preferences of the actors.

Answer:

QUESTION 140

A theater teacher is planning to direct a play set in the Elizabethan era of England. Which aspect of the production should be given the most attention to ensure historical accuracy?

    A.   The language and dialogue used by the characters.
    B.   The incorporation of modern technology and special effects.
    C.   The inclusion of contemporary dance and music styles.
    D.   The portrayal of characters with modern attitudes and beliefs.

Answer:

QUESTION 141

In a theater class exploring different historical periods, which activity would be most effective in helping students understand the essence of Ancient Greek theater?

    A.   Watching a modern movie based on an Ancient Greek play.
    B.   Engaging in a debate about the influence of Ancient Greek theater on contemporary drama.
    C.   Participating in a mask-making workshop to learn about the significance of masks in Greek theater.
    D.   Reading academic articles about the history of Ancient Greek theater.

Answer:

QUESTION 142

During the construction of a theater set, the theater teacher notices that some materials are not fire-retardant. What action should the teacher take to ensure the safety of the production?

    A.   Continue with the construction, ensuring that the materials are treated with a fire-retardant spray before the show.
    B.   Replace all non-fire-retardant materials with suitable fire-resistant alternatives.
    C.   Limit the use of non-fire-retardant materials to minor set elements away from potential hazards.
    D.   Consult with the local fire department for their approval before proceeding with the construction.

Answer:

QUESTION 143

As a theater teacher, one of your students is struggling to develop a coherent plot for their original stage play. What advice would you give to help them improve their storytelling?

    A. Suggest incorporating complex subplots to add depth to the main storyline.
    B. Advise them to introduce a large ensemble of characters to engage the audience.
    C. Encourage them to identify the protagonist's main objective and obstacles to create a strong central conflict.
    D. Recommend using elaborate stage effects and props to captivate the audience's attention.

Answer:

QUESTION 144

One of your theater students is interested in adapting a classic novel into a stage play. What is the most critical aspect they should consider during the adaptation process?

    A. Maintaining the original storyline and dialogues to preserve the essence of the novel.
    B. Condensing the narrative to fit the time constraints of a stage production.
    C. Introducing contemporary elements to make the play more relatable to a modern audience.
    D. Prioritizing visual spectacle and grand set designs to enhance the theatrical experience.

Answer:

QUESTION145

As a theater teacher, you want to encourage your students to generate creative ideas for their original plays. Which technique would you recommend to help them explore the depth of their characters?

    A. Conducting extensive historical research to create authentic character backgrounds.
    B. Utilizing improvisation exercises where students act out various scenarios as their characters.
    C. Assigning students to write detailed biographies for each character.
    D. Asking students to analyze classic plays and apply similar character archetypes to their own works.

Answer:

QUESTION 146

Your theater students are struggling to generate unique and compelling story ideas for their playmaking assignment. What approach would you recommend to help spark their creativity?

    A. Assigning them specific themes or topics to explore in their plays.
    B. Encouraging them to adapt popular films or books into original stage plays.
    C. Organizing brainstorming sessions where students can freely share and build upon each other's ideas.
    D. Providing pre-written plot outlines and asking students to expand on them with original characters and settings.

Answer:

QUESTION 147

As a theater teacher, you notice that one of your students' plays lacks a clear theme and message. What guidance would you offer to help them strengthen the script's communication of ideas and feelings?

    A. Suggest introducing more humor and lighthearted moments to engage the audience.
    B. Advise them to focus on creating visually striking stage settings to convey emotions effectively.
    C. Encourage them to explore the characters' inner conflicts and desires to develop a meaningful theme.
    D. Recommend adding complex plot twists to keep the audience intrigued throughout the play.

Answer:

QUESTION 148

One of your theater students has written a play with a complex plot involving multiple storylines. They seek advice on structuring the script effectively. What approach would you recommend to help them manage the complexity of their play?

A. Incorporate flashbacks and non-linear storytelling to add intrigue and depth.
B. Merge some of the storylines to create a more straightforward narrative.
C. Use a clear timeline and signpost events to guide the audience through the various storylines.
D. Focus on visual effects and set designs to distract the audience from the complexity of the plot.

Answer:

QUESTION 149

In a theater class exploring different dramatic styles, you want to introduce the concept of "absurd theater" to your students. Which play would be most suitable to exemplify this dramatic style?

A. "Romeo and Juliet" by William Shakespeare.
B. "The Importance of Being Earnest" by Oscar Wilde.
C. "Waiting for Godot" by Samuel Beckett.
D. "Death of a Salesman" by Arthur Miller.

Answer:

QUESTION 150

In designing a set for a Shakespearean tragedy, the production team is faced with the challenge of creating a realistic representation of a grand palace. Which principle of design should they prioritize to effectively convey the setting's grandeur?

A. Symmetry and Balance
B. Repetition and Rhythm
C. Contrast and Emphasis
D. Unity and Harmony

Answer:

QUESTION 151

During the Renaissance era, theater played a significant role in achieving which of the following societal purposes?

A. Preserving Oral Traditions
B. Promoting Religious Dogma
C. Encouraging Political Activism
D. Exploring Psychological Realism

Answer:

QUESTION 152

During rehearsals for a modern theatrical production, the director notices that the actors are struggling with maintaining proper vocal projection and clarity of speech. Which basic element of theatrical performance should the director focus on improving?

A. Blocking and Staging
B. Costume and Makeup
C. Lighting and Sound
D. Diction and Voice

Answer:

QUESTION 153

In a physical theater performance that relies heavily on gestures and movements to convey emotions and tell a story, which basic element of theatrical performance takes precedence?

A. Script and Dialogue
B. Music and Sound Effects
C. Lighting and Visual Effects
D. Movement and Gesture

Answer:

QUESTION 154

In a theater festival featuring various dramatic forms, a one-act play is presented that centers around a single intense conflict, involves a small cast, and typically concludes with an unresolved ending. Which type of dramatic form is being showcased?

A. Tragedy
B. Farce
C. Melodrama
D. Absurdist Theater

Answer:

QUESTION 155

During a discussion about theatrical forms, a theater teacher explains that Commedia dell'arte is characterized by its use of stock characters, improvisation, and physical comedy. Which type of dramatic form is being described?

A. Expressionism
B. Naturalism
C. Realism
D. Commedia dell'arte

Answer:

QUESTION 156

In a theater history class, students are studying the Elizabethan era of theater. One student asks how actors of that time managed to perform effectively in large open-air theaters without modern amplification. What key characteristic of Elizabethan acting should the teacher emphasize as a technique that allowed actors to project their voices?

A. Method Acting
B. Emotional Memory
C. Rhetorical Delivery
D. Stanislavski System

Answer:

QUESTION 157

During a discussion on historical acting styles, a theater teacher mentions that in Kabuki theater, actors often employ elaborate and stylized movements to express emotions. Which aspect of Kabuki acting does this description highlight?

A. Realism and Naturalism
B. Emotional Recall
C. Physical Exaggeration
D. Subtextual Analysis

Answer:

QUESTION 158

In a workshop focusing on modern actor training, students are encouraged to explore their own personal experiences and emotions to enhance their performances. Which prominent acting method or technique aligns with this approach?

A. Meisner Technique
B. Suzuki Method
C. Viewpoints
D. Grotowski's Poor Theater

Answer:

QUESTION 159

A group of actors is participating in a workshop that involves precise physical movements, attention to breath, and a focus on spatial awareness to develop ensemble performances. Which method of actor training is being implemented in this workshop?

A. Chekhov Technique
B. Laban Movement Analysis
C. Michael Chekhov Technique
D. Uta Hagen's Approach

Answer:

QUESTION 160

In a theater history class, students are studying the works of Anton Chekhov. A student asks why Chekhov's plays are often described as containing both humor and deep introspection. What aspect of Chekhov's writing style contributes to this unique combination?

A. Absurdist Dialogue
B. Prolific Monologues
C. Subtextual Patterning
D. Subtextual Layering

Answer:

QUESTION 161

During a discussion on playwrights and their impact, a theater teacher explains how Bertolt Brecht's plays often utilize alienation effects to prevent emotional identification with characters. What is the primary purpose of this technique in Brechtian theater?

A. Encouraging Emotional Catharsis
B. Fostering Escapist Entertainment
C. Promoting Political Engagement
D. Achieving Psychological Realism

Answer:

QUESTION 162

In a lecture on European theater history, the instructor discusses the emergence of "Theatre of the Absurd." Which key element characterizes this theatrical movement?

A. Rational Plot Structure
B. Linear Chronology
C. Logical Dialogue
D. Surreal and Illogical Situations

Answer:

QUESTION 163

A theater director is exploring the concept of "epic theater" developed by Bertolt Brecht. What is the primary intention of Brecht's epic theater in contrast to traditional dramatic forms?

    A.   Encouraging Emotional Immersion
    B.   Facilitating Cathartic Experiences
    C.   Prompting Audience Empathy
    D.   Promoting Critical Reflection

Answer:

QUESTION 164

What is a crucial aspect of adapting a stage play from one medium to another?

    A.   Maintaining the original dialogue and plot structure as closely as possible.
    B.   Altering the setting and characters to fit the new medium's requirements.
    C.   Reimagining the themes and messages of the original play.
    D.   Removing any elements that might be difficult to translate into the new medium.

Answer:

QUESTION 165

What is a key principle to consider when writing a stage play with multiple storylines and characters?

    A.   Keep the subplots unrelated to the main plot to avoid confusion.
    B.   Intertwine the storylines to create connections and thematic unity.
    C.   Focus solely on one central character to maintain clarity.
    D.   Avoid using supporting characters to prevent distractions from the main plot.

Answer:

QUESTION 166

Which technique involves actors spontaneously creating scenes and dialogue without a pre-established script?

    A.   Playmaking
    B.   Self-scripting
    C.   Improvisation
    D.   Multiple methods of research/information gathering

Answer:

QUESTION 167

When using multiple methods of research and information gathering for generating ideas, what does this process involve?

    A.   Relying solely on personal experiences and observations.
    B.   Utilizing only written materials such as books and articles.
    C.   Combining various sources, including interviews, fieldwork, and historical documents.
    D.   Focusing exclusively on fictional sources for creative inspiration.

Answer:

QUESTION 168

Which element of a script primarily drives the overall storyline and events?

    A.   Characters
    B.   Setting
    C.   Plot
    D.   Theme

Answer:

QUESTION 169

In a script, what is the function of the theme?

    A.   To describe the physical attributes of the characters and setting.
    B.   To establish the time and place in which the play is set.
    C.   To convey the central message or underlying idea of the play.
    D.   To outline the sequence of events and actions in the story.

Answer:

QUESTION 170

Which dramatic style is characterized by exaggerated and distorted physicality and emotions?

    A.   Realism
    B.   Absurdism
    C.   Expressionism
    D.   Naturalism

Answer:

QUESTION 171

Which dramatic form typically involves a series of short, unrelated scenes or vignettes without a traditional linear narrative?

    A.   Tragedy
    B.   Comedy
    C.   Farce
    D.   Sketch

Answer:

QUESTION 172

In Renaissance-era acting, what was the primary gender convention regarding actors on stage?

    A.   Women were allowed to perform only in comedic roles.
    B.   Men portrayed both male and female characters.
    C.   Women were prohibited from acting in any capacity.
    D.   Men were only allowed to perform in serious and tragic roles.

Answer:

QUESTION 173

Which historical style of acting emphasized a strong connection between the performer's emotions and the character portrayed?

- A. Melodrama
- B. Commedia dell'arte
- C. Kabuki
- D. Stanislavski's Method

Answer:

QUESTION 174

Which acting technique emphasizes physical actions and objectives to develop a character's motivation and behavior?

- A. Meisner Technique
- B. Viewpoints
- C. Grotowski Method
- D. Laban Movement Analysis

Answer:

QUESTION 175

What is a core principle of the Viewpoints technique used in contemporary actor training?

- A. Exploring the psychological depths of a character's backstory.
- B. Developing a strong vocal projection and enunciation.
- C. Breaking down the script into its basic structural elements.
- D. Understanding and utilizing spatial and movement concepts in performance.

Answer:

QUESTION 176

Which vocal technique involves controlling the pitch, volume, and pace of speech to effectively convey emotions and intentions?

- A. Pantomime
- B. Diction
- C. Voice Modulation
- D. Impulse Training

Answer:

QUESTION 177

What is the primary goal of physical warm-up exercises in actor training?

- A. To improve an actor's overall fitness and strength.
- B. To develop the ability to perform complex dance routines.
- C. To prevent injuries during physically demanding performances.
- D. To prepare an actor's body for the demands of the specific role or performance.

Answer:

QUESTION 178

Who is known for their significant contributions to the development of the regional theater movement in the United States?

A. Lee Strasberg
B. Tennessee Williams
C. Elia Kazan
D. Robert Edmond Jones

Answer:

QUESTION 179

What was a major development in American theatrical production during the 20th century that influenced storytelling and stagecraft?

A. The invention of the proscenium arch stage
B. The introduction of Method acting techniques
C. The establishment of the Actors Studio
D. The advent of multimedia and projection technology

Answer:

QUESTION 180

Who is considered a pioneer of African-American theater, known for their plays exploring themes of race, identity, and social issues in America?

A. August Wilson
B. Lorraine Hansberry
C. Langston Hughes
D. Amiri Baraka (LeRoi Jones)

Answer:

QUESTION 181

What prominent theme is often explored in contemporary American drama, focusing on the struggles and aspirations of ordinary individuals?

A. The pursuit of the American Dream
B. The supernatural and paranormal phenomena
C. The clash between different cultural identities
D. The depiction of historical events and figures

Answer:

QUESTION 182

What is a key characteristic of Absurdist plays in American drama?

A. Detailed historical settings and costumes
B. Linear and logical plotlines
C. Nihilistic and existential themes
D. Optimistic resolutions and happy endings

Answer:

QUESTION 183

Which theatrical movement emerged in response to the AIDS crisis and advocated for LGBTQ+ rights and visibility?

- A.   The Beat Generation movement
- B.   The Chicano theater movement
- C.   The Theatre of the Ridiculous
- D.   The New Queer Cinema movement

Answer:

QUESTION 184

What is a distinctive feature of traditional Japanese Noh theater?

- A.   Elaborate and ornate set designs
- B.   Lively and improvised dialogue
- C.   The use of masks to portray characters
- D.   Emphasis on slapstick comedy

Answer:

QUESTION 185

What is a prominent characteristic of Aboriginal Australian theater, often drawing from oral storytelling traditions?

- A.   Large ensembles with extensive choreography
- B.   The use of exclusively written scripts
- C.   Incorporating modern Western theatrical conventions
- D.   The absence of musical elements

Answer:

QUESTION 186

Which theatrical form from Africa combines storytelling, music, dance, and vibrant costumes to convey moral lessons and cultural values?

- A.   Noh theater
- B.   Commedia dell'arte
- C.   Griot performances
- D.   Kabuki theater

Answer:

QUESTION 187

In improvisation, what is the primary purpose of the "Yes, and..." rule?

- A.   To encourage actors to agree with everything their scene partner says.
- B.   To restrict actors from introducing new ideas in the scene.
- C.   To promote collaboration and build upon each other's contributions.
- D.   To ensure actors follow a predetermined script.

Answer:

QUESTION 188

What improvisation technique involves mimicking and exaggerating the physical actions and emotions of another actor?

    A. Status games
    B. Gibberish scenes
    C. Mirroring
    D. Word association

Answer:

QUESTION 189

When considering the stage layout for a production, what is the purpose of a thrust stage configuration?

    A. To enhance the intimacy and engagement with the audience.
    B. To allow for elaborate and expansive set designs.
    C. To separate the audience from the performers for a formal atmosphere.
    D. To maximize the seating capacity of the theater.

Answer:

QUESTION 190

What does blocking refer to in the context of staging a theatrical production?

    A. The use of props and set pieces to create a visually appealing stage.
    B. The positioning and movement of actors on the stage during a performance.
    C. The selection of appropriate costumes and makeup for the characters.
    D. The process of refining and rehearsing the play's script.

Answer:

QUESTION 191

When selecting a play for a school production, what factor should be given particular attention to ensure it is suitable for the intended audience?

    A. The play's popularity and recognition among theater professionals.
    B. The availability of skilled actors to portray the lead roles.
    C. The play's alignment with the school's educational objectives and values.
    D. The potential for commercial success and profitability.

Answer:

QUESTION 192

In the process of selecting a play for a community theater, what should be a primary consideration to ensure inclusivity and diversity representation?

    A. The play's potential to attract a large and diverse audience.
    B. The availability of actors who are already familiar with the play.
    C. The play's recognition and awards it has received from critics.
    D. The diversity of characters and themes portrayed in the play.

Answer:

QUESTION 193

In theatrical design, what does the principle of repetition involve?

    A. Using contrasting elements to create visual interest.
    B. Creating a sense of cohesion by repeating similar visual elements.
    C. Emphasizing a particular element to draw attention to it.
    D. Achieving a harmonious and balanced overall composition.

Answer:

QUESTION 194

How does the principle of emphasis work in theatrical design?

    A. It uses contrasting elements to create visual interest.
    B. It achieves a harmonious and balanced overall composition.
    C. It draws attention to a specific element or area on the stage.
    D. It creates a sense of cohesion by repeating similar visual elements.

Answer:

QUESTION 195

When designing the set for a tragic play, how might the principles of balance and contrast be applied?

    A. By creating a visually symmetrical and evenly distributed stage design.
    B. By using a variety of colors and shapes to create visual interest.
    C. By positioning characters at different heights to create dynamic staging.
    D. By incorporating elements of comedy and humor to lighten the mood.

Answer:

QUESTION 196

How might the principles of repetition and unity be utilized in costume design for an ensemble cast production?

    A. By using contrasting costumes to represent diverse character backgrounds.
    B. By repeating similar patterns and textures to create a cohesive look.
    C. By emphasizing individuality through unique and distinct costumes.
    D. By incorporating elements of different historical periods for visual variety.

Answer:

QUESTION 197

Which playwright is renowned for their exploration of the human condition through tragic plays, often depicting the consequences of pride and hubris?

    A. Anton Chekhov
    B. Samuel Beckett
    C. Euripides
    D. Caryl Churchill

Answer:

QUESTION 198

Which playwright is associated with the creation of farcical comedies that often satirize social conventions and human folly?

- A. Anton Chekhov
- B. Molière
- C. Samuel Beckett
- D. Caryl Churchill

Answer:

QUESTION 199

What is a distinguishing characteristic of American theater during the 20th century?

- A. The dominance of classical Greek tragedies in performances.
- B. The strict adherence to traditional theatrical conventions.
- C. The emergence of experimental and avant-garde theater movements.
- D. The exclusive focus on adaptations of European plays.

Answer:

QUESTION 200

How did the Harlem Renaissance influence American theater and dramatic literature?

- A. By promoting European classical plays over American works.
- B. By celebrating and elevating African-American artistic and cultural expression.
- C. By limiting the representation of diverse voices and experiences on stage.
- D. By discouraging the use of African-American themes in plays.

Answer:

QUESTION 201

What is a central theme often explored in existentialist drama?

- A. The pursuit of the American Dream
- B. The absurdity and meaninglessness of human existence
- C. The clash between different cultural identities
- D. The exploration of supernatural and paranormal phenomena

Answer:

QUESTION 202

What is a key characteristic of postmodern drama that distinguishes it from modernist drama?

- A. A rejection of experimental and non-linear narratives.
- B. A focus on portraying traditional and linear storytelling.
- C. A blending of various styles, genres, and cultural references.
- D. A preference for traditional theatrical conventions and realism.

Answer:

QUESTION 203

As a theater director, you are working on a classic play known for its powerful and emotional ending. During rehearsals, the lead actor suggests changing the ending to give it a more uplifting and optimistic tone. What should you, as the director, do?

A. Agree with the actor's suggestion and implement the new ending to make it more uplifting.
B. Consider the actor's suggestion but also discuss the original intention of the play's ending with the entire cast and crew.
C. Reject the actor's suggestion outright and maintain the original ending as written by the playwright.
D. Hold a vote among the cast and crew to decide whether to change the ending or keep it as it is.

Answer:

QUESTION 204

You are a theater producer faced with a limited budget for your upcoming production. One of the actors in the play is a well-known celebrity who demands a significantly higher salary than the rest of the cast. However, hiring this actor would exceed your budget. What should you do?

A. Negotiate with the well-known actor to lower their salary to fit within the budget.
B. Hire the well-known actor regardless of the budget constraints to attract more audiences.
C. Decide not to hire the well-known actor and cast someone else who fits the budget.
D. Seek additional funding or sponsors to accommodate the higher salary of the well-known actor.

Answer:

QUESTION 205

You are the lead designer for a theater production, and the director has requested a set design that includes elaborate moving parts and complex lighting effects. However, the budget for the production is limited, and executing the director's vision would require substantial resources. What should you do?

A. Inform the director that the requested set design and lighting effects are not feasible within the budget and suggest alternative options.
B. Attempt to create the complex set design and lighting effects, even if it means exceeding the budget.
C. Simplify the set design and lighting effects to fit within the budget while still maintaining the essence of the director's vision.
D. Ignore the budget constraints and proceed with the original design, hoping that the production will generate enough revenue to cover the costs.

Answer:

QUESTION 206

A theater teacher is planning a unit on Greek theater and its significant contributions to the history of drama. What approach should the teacher take to ensure a comprehensive understanding of Greek theater among the students?

A. Have the students read and analyze modern plays inspired by Greek mythology and themes.
B. Introduce the students to ancient Greek texts such as "Medea" and "Oedipus Rex" and discuss their cultural and historical context.
C. Conduct a field trip to a local theater production that showcases Greek theatrical techniques.
D. Organize a debate among students about the relevance of Greek theater in contemporary society.

Answer:

QUESTION 207

As a theater teacher working with children, you notice that one of your students is consistently shy and hesitant during drama activities. How can you encourage this student to become more actively involved in class?

A. Assign the student solo performances to build confidence and self-expression.
B. Ask the student's peers to provide constructive feedback and support during activities.
C. Incorporate group activities and ensemble-based exercises to create a supportive and inclusive environment.
D. Give the student written assignments instead of performance-based tasks to foster creativity and participation.

Answer:

QUESTION 208

A theater teacher wants to showcase the interdisciplinary aspects of theater to their students. What activity would best demonstrate the collaborative nature of theater with other art forms?

    A.   Having students write and perform original monologues.
    B.   Organizing a field trip to a local art gallery followed by a discussion on how visual art influences set design.
    C.   Teaching students basic music theory and composing original songs for a play.
    D.   Conducting a workshop on theater history and analyzing the impact of historical events on dramatic storytelling.

Answer:

QUESTION 209

As a theater director, you are working on a contemporary play with a diverse cast that explores sensitive and challenging social issues. During rehearsals, you notice that some actors are struggling to emotionally connect with their characters and deliver authentic performances. What should you, as the director, do?

    A.   Replace the actors who are having difficulty connecting with their characters to maintain the play's authenticity.
    B.   Organize a group therapy session for the actors to address their emotional challenges and improve their performances.
    C.   Schedule one-on-one sessions with each actor to discuss their characters and help them delve deeper into their emotions.
    D.   Modify the script to make the characters more relatable and less emotionally demanding for the actors.

Answer:

QUESTION 210

As a theater producer, you are planning to stage a musical that requires elaborate and costly set designs, costumes, and special effects. The musical has the potential to be a major hit, but it also carries a significant financial risk. What steps can you take to mitigate this risk while ensuring a successful production?

    A.   Increase ticket prices to cover the production's higher costs and potential financial risk.
    B.   Secure insurance to protect against potential losses in case the production is not financially successful.
    C.   Scale down the production's grand elements to reduce costs without compromising artistic integrity.
    D.   Partner with a local theater company to share the financial burden and resources for the production.

Answer:

QUESTION 211

As a set designer, you are tasked with creating a realistic and historically accurate set for a period drama set in ancient Rome. However, due to space limitations in the theater, you can't build grand and intricate sets. How can you overcome this challenge while maintaining the essence of the play's setting?

    A.   Use video projections to create virtual backgrounds and expand the sense of space and grandeur.
    B.   Build miniature models of key set elements to create an illusion of depth and scale.
    C.   Change the setting to a different historical period that allows for a simpler set design.
    D.   Rely on detailed and evocative costumes to transport the audience to ancient Rome without elaborate set pieces.

Answer:

QUESTION 212

A theater teacher is planning a unit on Japanese Noh theater for their advanced drama students. How can the teacher engage the students and encourage them to appreciate the unique qualities of Noh theater?

    A.   Have the students research and present on the history and key elements of Noh theater.
    B.   Organize a workshop where students can try on traditional Noh masks and costumes.
    C.   Show videos of Noh theater performances to illustrate its stylistic and symbolic aspects.
    D.   Assign students to adapt a famous Western play into a Noh-style performance.

Answer:

QUESTION 213

As a theater teacher, you want to introduce your students to the world of improvisational theater. How can you create a safe and supportive environment for students to explore improvisation?

    A.   Assign specific roles and scenarios to guide the students in their improvisations.
    B.   Start with simple improv games that focus on building trust and cooperation among the students.
    C.   Have the students watch professional improvisational performances before attempting it themselves.
    D.   Provide written scripts for students to memorize and then perform improvisations based on those scripts.

Answer:

QUESTION 214

A theater teacher wants to explore the relationship between theater and dance in a high school drama class. What activity would best demonstrate how these two art forms intersect?

    A.   Assigning students to write a play that incorporates dance sequences as integral storytelling elements.
    B.   Inviting a professional dance troupe to perform during a theater class and then discussing the similarities and differences between the two art forms.
    C.   Having students choreograph dance routines inspired by famous theatrical plays and present them to the class.
    D.   Organizing a collaborative project where theater students and dance students work together to create a performance that blends both art forms.

Answer:

QUESTION 215

As a theater director, you are preparing to stage a classic play known for its elaborate and grand set design. However, due to budget constraints, building the desired set seems challenging. What approach should you take to ensure the production maintains its artistic integrity while staying within the budget?

    A.   Seek sponsorship from local businesses to fund the elaborate set design.
    B.   Utilize creative lighting and minimalistic set pieces to evoke the desired atmosphere.
    C.   Reduce the number of performances to save on production costs.
    D.   Ask the cast and crew to volunteer their time and skills to cut down on expenses.

Answer:

QUESTION 216

As a theater director, you are staging a play that explores sensitive and emotionally intense themes. During rehearsals, you notice that some cast members are struggling with emotionally charged scenes, affecting the quality of their performances. What steps can you take as the director to support your actors and ensure the authenticity of their portrayals?

    A.   Replace the struggling actors with performers who can better handle the emotional scenes.
    B.   Encourage the cast to separate their emotions from the characters they portray.
    C.   Schedule individual sessions with the struggling actors to explore and understand their characters' emotional journeys.
    D.   Modify the script to lessen the emotional intensity of the scenes for the entire cast.

Answer:

QUESTION 217

As a theater director, you are working on a community theater production that involves a diverse group of volunteers, including amateur actors and professionals in the technical team. How can you foster effective collaboration and ensure a positive working environment?

    A.   Set strict hierarchies to maintain discipline and order among the volunteers.
    B.   Assign roles based on experience and skills, ensuring professionals take on leadership positions.
    C.   Encourage open communication and create a supportive atmosphere where everyone's contributions are valued.
    D.   Rely on the production's artistic vision and minimize the input from volunteers to avoid conflicts.

Answer:

QUESTION 218

As a theater director, you are collaborating with a local school to stage a production involving students as actors and community members as part of the production team. The school's staff expresses concern about the time commitment interfering with the students' academics. How can you address this concern and ensure a successful collaboration?

    A.   Suggest incorporating academic themes into the production to align with the students' coursework.
    B.   Organize regular rehearsals during school hours to minimize after-school time commitment.
    C.   Establish a clear rehearsal schedule and emphasize the importance of time management for both academics and theater.
    D.   Offer academic tutoring or support for students involved in the production.

Answer:

QUESTION 219

You are the stage manager for a large-scale theater production with a substantial cast and crew. During a tech rehearsal, you notice that the lighting cues are not synchronizing correctly with the actors' movements on stage. What should you, as the stage manager, do to address this issue?

    A.   Take over the lighting controls during the tech rehearsal to ensure the cues are executed correctly.
    B.   Discuss the issue with the lighting designer and collaborate on adjusting the cues to match the actors' movements.
    C.   Inform the director about the lighting issue and rely on them to communicate the necessary changes to the lighting designer.
    D.   Assign a crew member to manage the lighting cues separately, allowing you to focus on other aspects of the rehearsal.

Answer:

QUESTION 220

You are the producer of a theater company planning to stage a series of performances in different cities. To ensure the success of the tour, what should you, as the producer, prioritize in the planning and management of the production?

    A.   Selecting venues with the largest seating capacity to maximize audience attendance.
    B.   Minimizing production costs to maximize potential profits from ticket sales.
    C.   Establishing a clear and efficient communication system among the touring team and production staff.
    D.   Relying on local theater communities to handle the logistics in each city of the tour.

Answer:

QUESTION 221

You are evaluating a theater performance by a group of middle school students. One actor struggled with remembering their lines and frequently hesitated during the scenes. Despite this, their emotional expression and physical gestures were on point. What should be your primary consideration when evaluating this actor's performance?

    A. Deduct points for forgetting lines and hesitating.
    B. Focus on their emotional expression and physical gestures.
    C. Provide constructive feedback only on their line delivery.
    D. Evaluate them based on the overall group's performance.

Answer:

QUESTION 222

A theater class is collaborating with a music class to put on a musical production. The theater students are responsible for acting, while the music students are responsible for the live orchestra. During rehearsals, the two groups are having trouble synchronizing their timing. As a theater teacher, what approach should you take to address this issue?

    A. Ask the theater students to rehearse separately until their timing is perfect.
    B. Coordinate with the music teacher to hold joint rehearsals emphasizing timing.
    C. Advise the theater students to focus solely on their acting skills.
    D. Suggest canceling the live orchestra to avoid timing conflicts.

Answer:

QUESTION 223

In a theater history class, students are studying a play from the Elizabethan era. They are intrigued by the elaborate costumes and extravagant set designs used during that time. One student asks why theater in this era often showcased opulence and grandeur. How would you respond?

    A. Explain that opulence was a way to distract the audience from poor acting.
    B. Discuss how societal values and beliefs influenced artistic expression.
    C. Mention that elaborate sets were required for the acoustics of the time.
    D. Attribute it to the availability of modern technology for production.

Answer:

QUESTION 224

A group of high school students is tasked with writing a one-act play. They have developed an engaging plot with compelling characters, but their dialogue feels unnatural and forced. How would you guide them to improve their dialogue writing?

    A. Advise them to focus solely on refining the plot and characters.
    B. Suggest using complex vocabulary to enhance the dialogue.
    C. Encourage them to observe real conversations and incorporate natural speech patterns.
    D. Recommend adding lengthy monologues to develop character backgrounds.

Answer:

QUESTION 225

During a theater workshop, a student actor is struggling with portraying a character's emotions authentically in a dramatic scene. What technique would you suggest to help the student connect with the character's emotions?

    A.   Advise the student to focus on memorizing lines for a better performance.
    B.   Recommend analyzing the character's emotional journey and motivations.
    C.   Suggest distracting the mind with unrelated thoughts to appear more natural.
    D.   Tell the student to avoid emotional depth to prevent personal discomfort.

Answer:

QUESTION 226

You are assessing a kindergarten class's theater performance. One student appeared shy and hesitant on stage, while another displayed enthusiasm and confidence. How would you adjust your evaluation approach for these two students?

    A.   Focus solely on the confident student's performance.
    B.   Deduct points from both students for different levels of confidence.
    C.   Consider the shy student's effort and growth, emphasizing their participation.
    D.   Evaluate both students strictly based on memorization and line delivery.

Answer:

QUESTION 227

You are judging a high school theater competition. One group presented a traditional Shakespearean tragedy, while another performed a modern comedic play. How would you approach evaluating these diverse performances?

    A.   Favor the Shakespearean tragedy for its classic and timeless themes.
    B.   Focus solely on the comedic play for its contemporary relevance.
    C.   Evaluate each performance based on its genre's specific conventions and execution.
    D.   Deduct points from both performances due to their contrasting styles.

Answer:

QUESTION 228

A theater class is collaborating with a visual arts class to create a multimedia performance combining acting and projected artwork. However, the visual elements overpower the acting, causing the storyline to be overshadowed. How would you guide the students to balance these aspects effectively?

    A.   Advise the theater students to amplify their acting to match the visual elements.
    B.   Suggest reducing the visual elements to avoid overshadowing the acting.
    C.   Encourage both groups to collaborate and adjust their elements for harmony.
    D.   Instruct the visual arts students to completely remove their contributions.

Answer:

QUESTION 229

In a theater and history integration lesson, students are studying a historical play set during a significant period in world history. One student asks how the events of that time influenced the play's characters and plot. How would you guide the student to explore this connection?

    A.   Disregard the historical context and focus solely on the play's artistic aspects.
    B.   Explain that historical events have no impact on theatrical storytelling.
    C.   Encourage the student to research the historical period and draw parallels to the play.
    D.   Suggest skipping the historical study to avoid complicating the interpretation.

Answer:

QUESTION 230

You are teaching a theater appreciation class, and a student asks why studying ancient Greek theater is relevant today. How would you explain the enduring significance of ancient Greek theater in relation to the humanities?

    A. Describe how ancient Greek theater solely focused on entertainment.
    B. Explain that ancient Greek theater has no relevance in contemporary society.
    C. Discuss how ancient Greek theater explored universal human themes and influenced modern storytelling.
    D. Suggest that ancient Greek theater is irrelevant due to its cultural differences.

Answer:

QUESTION 231

In a theater and philosophy seminar, students are debating whether theater can serve as a form of philosophical inquiry. Some argue that theater merely provides entertainment, while others believe it can provoke thought and introspection. How would you contribute to this discussion?

    A. Support the notion that theater has no connection to philosophy.
    B. Emphasize that theater can only be appreciated for its aesthetic qualities.
    C. Discuss how theater often raises thought-provoking s and challenges assumptions.
    D. Suggest that philosophical inquiry is solely limited to written texts.

Answer:

QUESTION 232

A group of middle school students is writing a play, and they're struggling with creating a cohesive storyline. Some students want to incorporate multiple unrelated plotlines. How would you guide them to improve their play's structure?

    A. Encourage them to keep the unrelated plotlines for added complexity.
    B. Suggest they eliminate all but one plotline for simplicity.
    C. Explain the importance of a unified central theme and consistent plotlines.
    D. Advise them to incorporate fantastical elements to connect the plotlines.

Answer:

QUESTION 233

During a playwriting workshop, a student asks why character development is essential in a well-written play. How would you respond to emphasize the significance of well-developed characters?

    A. State that character development is unnecessary if the plot is exciting.
    B. Explain that audiences don't care about characters; they care about the action.
    C. Discuss how well-developed characters create emotional connections and drive the plot.
    D. Suggest that character development is only important for novels, not plays.

Answer:

QUESTION 234

In an acting workshop, a student struggles with portraying a character's conflicting emotions convincingly. They find it challenging to express both joy and sadness in a single scene. How would you guide the student to effectively convey these complex emotions?

    A. Suggest they focus solely on one emotion to avoid confusion.
    B. Advise them to avoid showing conflicting emotions altogether.
    C. Encourage them to explore how the character's circumstances lead to these emotions.
    D. Recommend ignoring the emotional aspect and concentrating on physical actions.

Answer:

Chapter 2 – Answers and Explanations

QUESTION 1

Answer: B

Explanation: Tragicomedy is a genre that combines elements of both tragedy and comedy. It alternates between moments of intense sorrow and lighthearted humor, creating a unique blend of emotions that allows the play to explore profound themes while also providing moments of relief and laughter.

QUESTION 2

Answer: C

Explanation: In theater, the arrangement of objects, actors, and scenery within the performance area is a fundamental aspect of design. This arrangement is known as "space." It involves how elements are positioned in relation to each other and the overall stage.

QUESTION 3

Answer: D

Explanation: Contrast is a design principle that involves placing different elements together to create visual or conceptual interest. It helps draw attention to specific aspects within a design by highlighting their differences.

QUESTION 4

Answer: B

Explanation: The Baroque period in theater history, characterized by its ornate and extravagant style, featured opulent costumes, intricate set designs, and dramatic performances that emphasized grandeur and spectacle.

QUESTION 5

Answer: B

Explanation: Expressionism is a theatrical style that emerged in the early 20th century, focusing on the inner emotions and subjective experiences of characters. It often employs symbolism, non-linear storytelling, and distorted visuals to convey psychological states.

QUESTION 6

Answer: C

Explanation: Producing in theater involves the overall management of a production, including financial planning, scheduling, hiring, and logistical coordination to ensure the successful execution of the performance.

QUESTION 7

Answer: A

Explanation: Pre-production is the phase of theater production where planning and preparation take place before rehearsals begin. Securing sponsorships, partnerships, and funding are important tasks during this phase to ensure the financial support needed for the production.

QUESTION 8

Answer: B

Explanation: Blocking refers to the detailed choreography of movements and positions of actors on stage. It's often outlined in a blocking notation or diagram to provide clear instructions for the actors and crew.

QUESTION 9

Answer: B

Explanation: Set design involves creating the physical environment and backdrop for a play. It includes the construction of the stage, props, and scenic elements that help establish the setting and atmosphere of the production.

QUESTION 10

Answer: B

Explanation: Costume designers create detailed sketches or renderings of costumes during the conceptual phase of design. These renderings visually communicate their ideas, providing a clear understanding of how the costumes will look on stage.

QUESTION 11

Answer: D

Explanation: Lighting design in theater is used to create specific moods, atmospheres, and visual effects that complement the performance. It can enhance the overall aesthetic and emotional impact of a production.

QUESTION 12

Answer: D

Explanation: Sophocles was a prominent ancient Greek playwright known for his contributions to Greek tragedy. His plays often explore themes of fate, morality, and the human condition.

QUESTION 13

Answer: D

Explanation: Henrik Ibsen is often credited with ushering in the era of modern drama with his realistic and socially relevant plays that delved into psychological and societal issues.

QUESTION 14

Answer: B

Explanation: Arthur Miller is a renowned American playwright whose works are known for their exploration of the American Dream, morality, and social issues. "Death of a Salesman" and "The Crucible" are among his well-known plays.

QUESTION 15

Answer: C

Explanation: Experiential learning involves active engagement and participation in the learning process through practical activities, allowing students to gain firsthand experience and insights.

QUESTION 16

Answer: D

Explanation: Theater education programs should provide material that is appropriate for the age and cognitive development of children. This ensures that the content is engaging, comprehensible, and aligned with their learning needs.

QUESTION 17

Answer: C

Explanation: Role-playing is a theater education technique where students take on different roles and engage in improvisation. This approach fosters creativity, empathy, and a deeper understanding of character development.

QUESTION 18

Answer: C

Explanation: Theater's interdisciplinary nature allows students to explore connections between theater and other subjects like history, literature, psychology, and more. This integration enhances their understanding of both theater and various academic disciplines.

QUESTION 19

Answer: C

Explanation: Theater often requires actors, designers, and crew members to collaborate closely, fostering effective communication, problem-solving, and teamwork. These skills are valuable in various aspects of life beyond the stage.

QUESTION 20

Answer: D

Explanation: Studying theater encourages critical thinking by analyzing scripts, characters, and historical contexts. It also fosters empathy by immersing students in diverse perspectives and human experiences, enhancing their ability to understand and connect with others.

QUESTION 21

Answer: C

Explanation: Blocking refers to the process of planning and mapping out the movement and positions of actors on the stage during a theatrical production. It helps in ensuring that the actors' movements are coordinated and visually appealing, enhancing the overall storytelling and performance.

QUESTION 22

Answer: C

Explanation: A "cue-to-cue" rehearsal is an essential part of the rehearsal process in theater. It involves practicing specific portions of the production, focusing mainly on the scene changes and technical cues. It allows the crew and actors to become familiar with the timing and execution of technical elements, such as lighting, sound, and set changes.

QUESTION 23

Answer: C

Explanation: Theater plays a vital role in promoting cultural understanding and empathy by presenting diverse perspectives and human experiences on stage. Through the portrayal of different characters and their stories, theater allows audiences to empathize with the struggles, joys, and complexities of individuals from various backgrounds, fostering a deeper appreciation for human diversity and empathy towards others.

QUESTION 24

Answer: C

Explanation: Theater is considered a form of storytelling within the humanities because it integrates various artistic elements, such as acting, set design, music, and lighting, to convey narratives and evoke emotions. Through this multidimensional approach, theater brings stories to life on stage, making it a powerful medium for expressing human experiences and exploring complex themes.

QUESTION 25

Answer: C

Explanation: Theater is closely tied to historical and cultural contexts in the humanities by reflecting the social and political climate of its time. Throughout history, theater has often served as a platform to address and comment on current events, societal norms, and cultural values. This reflection allows theater to become a lens through which audiences can understand and analyze the historical and cultural nuances of specific periods.

QUESTION 26

Answer: C

Explanation: In theater production, the term "ensemble" refers to a group of actors working collaboratively as a cohesive unit. The ensemble approach emphasizes the importance of collective creativity and teamwork, where each actor contributes to the overall performance and storytelling, rather than focusing solely on individual performances or star power.

QUESTION 27

Answer: C

Explanation: Theatrical improvisation plays a crucial role in actor training as it enhances spontaneity, creativity, and adaptability on stage. By engaging in improvisational exercises, actors learn to think on their feet, respond to unexpected situations, and explore different character choices, ultimately improving their overall performance skills and ability to collaborate effectively with fellow actors.

QUESTION 28

Answer: B

Explanation: In theater, the term "blocking" refers to the process of mapping out the movement and positions of actors on stage during a theatrical production. The director and the stage manager work together to plan and organize the actors' movements, ensuring a visually cohesive and compelling performance that enhances the storytelling.

QUESTION 29

Answer: C

Explanation: The exposition in a play's dramatic structure serves the purpose of providing background information and context to the audience. It introduces the characters, their relationships, and the setting, setting the stage for the main conflict and helping the audience understand the events that follow.

QUESTION 30

Answer: C

Explanation: A well-structured play is distinguished from one with weak dramatic structure by the effective organization of plot events and their impact on the audience. A strong dramatic structure ensures a logical flow of events, engaging storytelling, and emotional resonance, while weak dramatic structure may result in a disjointed and less impactful narrative.

QUESTION 31

Answer: C

Explanation: In a play's dramatic structure, the resolution phase reveals the outcome of the main conflict and ties up loose ends, providing closure to the story. On the other hand, the climax is the turning point of the play, where tension and conflicts reach their peak, leading to a significant change in the story's direction. These two phases serve different purposes in the overall narrative progression.

QUESTION 32

Answer: D

Explanation: The "subtext" in acting refers to the underlying thoughts and emotions that are not explicitly stated in the dialogue. It is the unspoken feelings and intentions of the character that actors must convey through their performance, adding depth and authenticity to their portrayal.

QUESTION 33

Answer: C

Explanation: Active listening is crucial in acting as it enables actors to respond genuinely and spontaneously to their fellow actors' lines and actions. It enhances the authenticity of the scene, fosters natural interactions between characters, and contributes to the overall believability of the performance.

QUESTION 34

Answer: C

Explanation: "Sense memory" in acting techniques refers to the process of recalling physical sensations associated with a specific emotional memory from the actor's own life. By tapping into these real-life sensory experiences, actors can evoke genuine emotions in their performances, contributing to the authenticity and depth of their characters' emotions.

QUESTION 35

Answer: C

Explanation: The director plays a vital role in shaping the visual elements of a theatrical production by collaborating with designers. They work together to create a unified and cohesive visual concept for the production, encompassing set design, lighting, costumes, and other visual elements, to support and enhance the overall storytelling and theme of the play.

QUESTION 36

Answer: C

Explanation: The primary objective of a director during the rehearsal process is to guide and shape the actors' performances. They work with the actors to develop their characters, emotions, and interactions, ensuring that the performances align with the director's vision for the production.

QUESTION 37

Answer: C

Explanation: A director can effectively manage conflicts and creative differences among the production team by encouraging open communication and collaborative problem-solving. By fostering an environment where team members feel heard and valued, the director can address conflicts constructively, allowing for creative ideas to be explored while maintaining a unified vision for the production.

QUESTION 38

Answer: C

Explanation: Robert Wilson, an American theater director, is known for his innovative work in "total theater," which combines various elements like movement, design, and music to create immersive and visually stunning productions. His avant-garde approach has had a significant impact on modern theater and performance art.

QUESTION 39

Answer: B

Explanation: The Great Depression, an economic crisis that occurred in the 1930s, greatly influenced American theater. During this period, playwrights and theater artists became more socially conscious, addressing relevant political and social issues in their works. The emergence of politically relevant plays reflected the struggles and concerns of the American people during that time.

QUESTION 40

Answer: C

Explanation: Noh is a traditional Japanese theatrical form that dates back to the 14th century. It is known for its use of colorful masks, elaborate costumes, and stylized movements. Noh plays often revolve around themes of supernatural beings, historical events, and legends.

QUESTION 41

Answer: D

Explanation: Griot is a theatrical tradition from Africa, particularly West Africa, known for its vibrant drumming, dance, and storytelling performances. Griots are oral historians and storytellers who pass down cultural and historical knowledge through their performances, playing a significant role in preserving African traditions and heritage.

QUESTION 42

Answer: C

Explanation: Obtaining performance licenses and royalties for a theatrical production is essential to secure the legal rights to perform a copyrighted work. This ensures that the playwright or rights holder receives appropriate compensation for the use of their intellectual property and protects the production from copyright infringement claims.

QUESTION 43

Answer: C

Explanation: A performance contract, also known as an artist agreement or employment contract, outlines the terms and conditions of the agreement between a theater producer and the creative team involved in the production. It includes details regarding compensation, responsibilities, rehearsal schedules, and other important aspects of the collaboration. This document ensures clarity and mutual understanding between the parties involved and helps prevent potential disputes during the production process.

QUESTION 44

Answer: A

Explanation: The scenery in a theatrical performance serves the primary function of creating a backdrop for the actors' movements. It includes the set design, props, and stage elements that help establish the setting and environment in which the characters interact and perform.

QUESTION 45

Answer: C

Explanation: In theater, "blocking" refers to the process of planning and mapping out the actors' movements and positions on stage. It is a critical stage direction that ensures the actors' movements are well-coordinated, visually appealing, and aligned with the storytelling and overall direction of the play.

QUESTION 46

Answer: B

Explanation: The primary purpose of using makeup in theatrical performances is to ensure the actors are recognizable to the audience, especially from a distance. The makeup helps define the characters' features, expressions, and age, enhancing their visibility and supporting the storytelling for the audience.

QUESTION 47

Answer: C

Explanation: The sound designer's role in a theatrical production involves designing and coordinating all sound-related elements, including music, sound effects, and live or recorded sound. They work closely with the director and production team to create a soundscape that complements and enhances the overall experience of the performance.

QUESTION 48

Answer: C

Explanation: Backstory involves developing a rich history for a character, which informs their actions and choices within the play.

QUESTION 49

Answer: C

Explanation: Gesture refers to the physical movements and actions a character employs to express their emotions and intentions.

QUESTION 50

Answer: C

Explanation: This principle encourages actors to accept and expand on each other's contributions, fostering a collaborative and creative environment.

QUESTION 51

Answer: A

Explanation: Mime is a form of improvisation where actors communicate through body language and movement rather than words.

QUESTION 52

Answer: D

Explanation: Realism in drama aims to depict life and society in a truthful and authentic manner, often addressing social issues and portraying ordinary characters.

QUESTION 53

Answer: D

Explanation: Morality is a significant theme in drama that delves into ethical s and the choices characters make in various situations.

QUESTION 54

Answer: C

Explanation: Romantic drama focused on emotional and psychological aspects, often portraying characters driven by powerful passions and facing tragic consequences.

QUESTION 55

Answer: A

Explanation: This approach engages students in active participation, allowing them to connect with the material on a personal level and enhance their understanding.

QUESTION 56

Answer: C

Explanation: Devising in drama education empowers students to collaborate, brainstorm, and collectively create their own performances, fostering creativity and teamwork.

QUESTION 57

Answer: D

Explanation: Rubrics provide clear guidelines for evaluating performances and enable students to assess the quality of theatrical work based on predetermined criteria.

QUESTION 58

Answer: A

Explanation: Children in the pre-operational stage (ages 2 to 7) exhibit a rich imagination and are drawn to dramatic play, often immersing themselves in creative and fantastical scenarios.

QUESTION 59

Answer: C

Explanation: Drama activities allow adolescents to explore and understand different emotions, perspectives, and experiences, thereby enhancing their ability to empathize with others.

QUESTION 60

Answer: C

Explanation: Adolescents often experience role confusion as they explore different identities and roles in drama, contributing to their personal and artistic growth.

QUESTION 61

Answer: C

Explanation: It's essential to choose a play that students can connect with, as it enhances their engagement and understanding, allowing them to explore themes that are relatable and meaningful.

QUESTION 62

Answer: B

Explanation: Choosing a play with manageable technical demands, such as fewer or simpler set changes, is important to ensure that the production can be effectively staged with the available resources.

QUESTION 63

Answer: B

Explanation: Melodrama is known for its heightened emotions, moral contrasts, and often simplified characterizations, making it easily accessible to audiences.

QUESTION 64

Answer: A

Explanation: Farce is characterized by exaggerated situations, physical comedy, and humorous misunderstandings, often presenting a critique of societal norms and conventions.

QUESTION 65

Answer: B

Explanation: Cultural factors, such as traditions, customs, and societal norms, play a significant role in theater. They can influence the visual aspects of a play, such as costumes and set designs, as well as the language used by the characters, making the performance more authentic and relatable to the intended audience.

QUESTION 66

Answer: B

Explanation: The political climate of a region can have a profound impact on theater. Governments or authorities may censor plays or themes that challenge the status quo or criticize the ruling regime. This censorship can limit artistic expression and force playwrights and directors to navigate sensitive topics carefully.

QUESTION 67

Answer: C

Explanation: Economic factors can create barriers to access for theater. To address this, theaters may offer discounts and subsidies to make tickets more affordable for low-income individuals and students, thereby promoting inclusivity and diversifying their audience.

QUESTION 68

Answer: A

Explanation: In Greek classical theater, the chorus played a central role in the performance, offering commentary, interacting with characters, and providing background information. In modern theater, the chorus is not a common feature, and its functions are often fulfilled through other means, such as dialogue or monologues by individual characters.

QUESTION 69

Answer: D

Explanation: "Verisimilitude" in Renaissance theater refers to the attempt to create a sense of realism while understanding that artistic liberties are necessary for dramatic purposes. While settings and characters may be based on reality, they can be heightened or altered to serve the play's themes and plot effectively.

QUESTION 70

Answer: D

Explanation: The "Theatre of the Absurd" movement, exemplified by playwrights like Samuel Beckett, challenged traditional theater by rejecting conventional storytelling and presenting a fragmented and absurd portrayal of the human experience. It focused on the meaningless and chaotic aspects of life, breaking away from established theatrical norms.

QUESTION 71

Answer: C

Explanation: Anton Chekhov's plays often delved into the complexities of human existence and the search for meaning in life. Themes of existentialism, the passage of time, and the characters' inner struggles were recurrent elements in his works.

QUESTION 72

Answer: A

Explanation: "Tartuffe" is a famous play by Molière that satirizes religious hypocrisy and fanaticism. The character Tartuffe is a religious imposter who deceives the gullible Orgon and exposes the flaws in blind religious devotion.

QUESTION 73

Answer: C

Explanation: "Top Girls" by Caryl Churchill challenges traditional storytelling by intertwining multiple historical periods and perspectives. The play features anachronistic scenes and brings together characters from different time periods to examine the complexities of feminism and women's roles throughout history.

QUESTION 74

Answer: B

Explanation: Bertolt Brecht believed in distancing the audience from emotional identification with the characters. He introduced the concept of "alienation" (Verfremdungseffekt) in his productions to remind the audience that they are watching a play and should critically engage with the social and political issues presented, rather than becoming emotionally absorbed in the story.

QUESTION 75

Answer: B

Explanation: During the Renaissance, theaters started using movable sets and wagons, which allowed for more elaborate and dynamic stage designs. These innovations enabled scene changes to be executed swiftly, contributing to the development of more complex and visually impressive theatrical productions.

QUESTION 76

Answer: C

Explanation: "Theatre of Cruelty," as envisioned by Antonin Artaud, aimed to evoke primal emotions and confront the audience with intense and visceral experiences. It rejected conventional storytelling and sought to challenge established perceptions of reality, emphasizing the power of raw and elemental emotions in theatrical performances.

QUESTION 77

Answer: B

Explanation: Irish playwrights like Sean O'Casey and Brian Friel often explore themes related to Ireland's history of revolutionary nationalism, political upheaval, and struggles for independence. Their works reflect the turbulent social and political landscape of their homeland.

QUESTION 78

Answer: B

Explanation: Henrik Ibsen is known as the "father of realism" in theater. He popularized this theatrical style in the late 19th century, particularly in his play "A Doll's House." Realism sought to portray everyday life and human behavior truthfully, focusing on realistic characters and settings.

QUESTION 79

Answer: D

Explanation: Surrealism was heavily influenced by Sigmund Freud's theories on the subconscious mind and dreams. Surrealist playwrights sought to create illogical and dreamlike worlds on stage, exploring the hidden depths of the human psyche and challenging conventional reality.

QUESTION 80

Answer: C

Explanation: When adapting a classic novel for the stage, it is essential to retain the core themes and character motivations that make the story resonate with audiences. While some adjustments may be necessary for theatricality, maintaining the essence of the original work ensures that the adaptation remains faithful to the source material.

QUESTION 81

Answer: B

Explanation: Monologues allow characters to express their innermost thoughts, desires, and emotions directly to the audience. By using monologues strategically, playwrights can provide deeper insights into characters' complexities, creating richer and more multidimensional personas on stage.

QUESTION 82

Answer: C

Explanation: Understanding dramatic structure is essential in playwriting because it provides a coherent framework for organizing the plot's events and the emotional journey of the characters. It helps create a cohesive narrative and ensures that the play engages and resonates with the audience effectively.

QUESTION 83

Answer: B

Explanation: Improvisation in theater involves actors spontaneously creating scenes and dialogue without a predefined script. It can be used during rehearsals to explore different character dynamics, storylines, and emotions, thereby generating fresh ideas and enriching the playwriting process.

QUESTION 84

Answer: A

Explanation: When writing a historical period play, conducting interviews with contemporary experts, such as historians or specialists in that specific era, can provide valuable insights and ensure historical accuracy. This firsthand knowledge can add depth and authenticity to the play's setting, characters, and themes.

QUESTION 85

Answer: B

Explanation: Playmaking involves a collaborative approach to generating ideas for a stage play. By encouraging group discussions and brainstorming sessions, each collaborator can contribute unique perspectives, leading to a more comprehensive exploration of ideas and fostering creativity within the team.

QUESTION 86

Answer: C

Explanation: The setting of a play not only provides a physical space for the characters to inhabit but also serves as a backdrop that enhances the mood and atmosphere of the production. The choice of setting can significantly impact how ideas and emotions are communicated to the audience.

QUESTION 87

Answer: C

Explanation: The theme of a play serves as the underlying message or central idea that the playwright wants to convey to the audience. It provides a cohesive purpose for the entire script and guides the development of characters, conflicts, and plot events.

QUESTION 88

Answer: C

Explanation: Foreshadowing involves dropping subtle hints or clues about future events in the play. This technique creates anticipation and intrigue, engaging the audience's interest as they eagerly await the unfolding of the story and its eventual resolutions.

QUESTION 89

Answer: C

Explanation: In theatrical production, effective communication is crucial for a successful collaboration. Establishing open and respectful channels of communication fosters a positive and supportive environment, allowing team members to express ideas, concerns, and feedback freely, leading to better creative outcomes and teamwork.

QUESTION 90

Answer: C

Explanation: Theater teachers can foster a sense of community involvement in a school production by actively engaging parents, teachers, and students in different aspects of the production. Involving the community creates a supportive and inclusive atmosphere, promotes collaboration, and encourages a broader appreciation for theater within the school.

QUESTION 91

Answer: B

Explanation: The stage manager is primarily responsible for coordinating and overseeing the technical and artistic aspects of a theatrical production. They work closely with the director, actors, and production staff to ensure that rehearsals run smoothly, technical elements are well-coordinated, and the show is executed as planned.

QUESTION 92

Answer: C

Explanation: The theatrical producer's primary role is to manage the financial and business aspects of the production. This includes securing funding, budgeting, organizing contracts, marketing, and overseeing the overall financial success of the show.

QUESTION 93

Answer: C

Explanation: For high school productions, it is essential to consider the age-appropriateness of the content. The selected play should be suitable for both the student actors' abilities and the audience's maturity level, ensuring a positive and responsible theatrical experience.

QUESTION 94

Answer: D

Explanation: In community theaters with limited financial resources, one of the most significant considerations in selecting a play is the royalty fees and overall production costs. Opting for plays with lower royalty fees and manageable production costs can help ensure the financial feasibility and success of the production.

QUESTION 95

Answer: C

Explanation: Obtaining performance rights or licenses for a play is crucial to protect against copyright infringement and potential legal disputes. It grants the production team the legal permission to perform the play and ensures compliance with copyright laws and intellectual property rights.

QUESTION 96

Answer: C

Explanation: Liability insurance for theatrical productions is necessary to protect against potential accidents, injuries, or property damage that may occur during rehearsals or performances. It provides financial coverage and protection for the theater producer in case of any unforeseen incidents or claims related to the production.

QUESTION 97

Answer: A

Explanation: Asking potential actors to perform a monologue is an effective approach during auditions to assess their artistic abilities. This allows theater teachers to evaluate the actors' acting skills, characterization, and emotional range, helping in making casting decisions for the production.

QUESTION 98

Answer: B

Explanation: When selecting a technical director for a theatrical production, the primary consideration should be their experience and knowledge in technical aspects of theater. Technical directors are responsible for overseeing various technical elements, such as lighting, sound, set design, and rigging, making their expertise and experience crucial for the success of the production.

QUESTION 99

Answer: C

Explanation: Creating a detailed production schedule is important to ensure the production runs on time and smoothly. It helps in coordinating rehearsals, technical preparations, and other production-related tasks, ensuring that everyone involved is aware of their roles and responsibilities and that the show is ready for its intended performance dates.

QUESTION 100

Answer: C

Explanation: A primary consideration when budgeting for a theatrical production is to keep production costs within financial constraints. Theater producers must balance expenses and revenue sources to ensure the production

QUESTION 101

Answer: C

Explanation: Expressionism is a dramatic style that emphasizes the emotional and psychological experiences of characters. It employs exaggerated and stylized movements and gestures to convey inner turmoil and subjective realities, often distorting reality for artistic effect.

QUESTION 102

Answer: D

Explanation: The thriller genre typically features elements of mystery, suspense, and unexpected plot twists that keep the audience on the edge of their seats. It focuses on creating tension and excitement as the plot unfolds, often involving themes of danger, crime, and intrigue.

QUESTION 103

Answer: C

Explanation: Expressionism in drama aimed to convey emotional and psychological states through distorted visuals and heightened language, reflecting the inner turmoil of characters.

QUESTION 104

Answer: D

Explanation: This theme often involves characters whose excessive pride or character flaws contribute to their tragic downfall, a common element in classical and modern tragedies.

QUESTION 105

Answer: D

Explanation: Elementary students are typically in the early stages of developing acting skills, and focusing on expressive body language helps build a strong foundation for future growth.

QUESTION 106

Answer: D

Explanation: Ensuring a safe environment for middle school students is paramount, and evaluating the practicality and safety of set design and props is a key consideration.

QUESTION 107

Answer: B

Explanation: Emotional recall involves drawing upon personal experiences and emotions to authentically portray a character's feelings and reactions.

QUESTION 108

Answer: C

Explanation: Improvisation is a valuable tool for actors to develop essential skills. It promotes quick thinking, adaptability to unexpected situations, and the ability to embody characters authentically. Improvisational exercises nurture creativity and expand an actor's range, making them more versatile and capable performers.

QUESTION 109

Answer: C

Explanation: Effective casting involves recognizing each actor's strengths and tailoring roles to showcase those strengths. By casting each actor in roles that align with their abilities, you can maximize their performances and contribute to a well-rounded production.

QUESTION 110

Answer: B

Explanation: Chemistry between actors can significantly enhance scenes, contributing to a more engaging performance. Utilizing this chemistry by casting the actor in a role that aligns with their strengths allows you to leverage their dynamic connection and elevate the overall quality of the production.

QUESTION 111

Answer: C

Explanation: Creating visual contrast between settings helps communicate the play's narrative and immerse the audience. Incorporating unique elements and props for each location enables the audience to differentiate between the cozy cottage and bustling city street, enhancing the overall storytelling experience.

QUESTION 112

Answer: C

Explanation: Balancing historical accuracy with practicality is crucial for a successful production. By combining historically accurate silhouettes with modern fabrics that provide comfort and ease of movement, the student can create costumes that honor the period while ensuring the actors' performance is not compromised.

QUESTION 113

Answer: C

Explanation: Cultural context deeply influences the characters' motivations, behaviors, and interactions, as well as the play's themes and underlying messages. Understanding the cultural backdrop allows actors and directors to make informed choices, ensuring a more authentic and insightful interpretation of the script.

QUESTION 114

Answer: C

Explanation: Symbolic elements add depth and layers to a script. Encouraging actors to delve into the metaphorical meanings allows them to infuse their performances with nuanced interpretations, creating a richer and more thought-provoking experience for the audience.

QUESTION 115

Answer: A

Explanation: The scene described, where a father conceals a dark secret during a family dinner, is characteristic of the play "Death of a Salesman" by Arthur Miller. In this play, the protagonist Willy Loman struggles with his identity and past mistakes, leading to a powerful and emotional family dynamic.

QUESTION 116

Answer: A

Explanation: Marlon Brando was a prominent American actor known for his influential method acting approach. He famously played Stanley Kowalski in the Broadway production of Tennessee Williams' "A Streetcar Named Desire," and his immersive performances greatly impacted American theatrical performance and production.

QUESTION 117

Answer: B

Explanation: "The Flick" by Annie Baker is a contemporary American drama that delves into the complexities of human connections in the digital age. Set in a small-town movie theater, the play explores themes of isolation, communication, and the impact of technology on relationships, making it a suitable choice for the drama teacher's exploration.

QUESTION 118

Answer: A

Explanation: Noh is a traditional Japanese theater form known for its stylized movements, masks, and use of historical or supernatural themes. It has a rich history and is performed with meticulous attention to detail, making it a significant representation of Asian dramatic literature and theater.

QUESTION 119

Answer: A

Explanation: Athol Fugard is a major playwright known for addressing apartheid and social issues in South Africa. "Master Harold and the Boys" is one of his notable plays, which explores the psychological consequences of racial discrimination and the human relationships affected by it.

QUESTION 120

Answer: C

Explanation: Jennifer Tipton is a prominent lighting designer known for her innovative use of light in theatrical productions. She has been recognized for integrating lighting as a storytelling element and creating visually striking stage environments that enhance the overall theatrical experience.

QUESTION 121

Answer: A

Explanation: Samuel Beckett is an influential playwright closely associated with the genre of absurdism. His plays, such as "Waiting for Godot" and "Endgame," are notable for their exploration of the human condition, existential themes, and the use of nonsensical situations to convey deeper meanings.

QUESTION 122

Answer: A

Explanation: Emotional recall, also known as affective memory or sense memory, is a technique introduced by Stanislavski to help actors access authentic emotions by drawing upon their personal emotional memories and experiences. This method enables actors to create more genuine and emotionally rich performances.

QUESTION 123

Answer: B

Explanation: "Alice in Wonderland" is a popular children's play based on Lewis Carroll's classic novel. It features a diverse cast of whimsical and memorable characters, providing ample opportunities for young students to explore different roles and showcase their creative talents in a fun and imaginative setting.

QUESTION 124

Answer: A

Explanation: The instructor is encouraging the improvisational technique known as "Environment Swap." In this technique, performers switch the setting or location of the scene while keeping the characters and basic premise intact. It challenges the actors to adapt quickly to new surroundings, enhancing their spontaneity and creativity during improvisation.

QUESTION 125

Answer: B

Explanation: The teacher is emphasizing the improvisational technique of "Pantomime." Pantomime involves using body movements and gestures to communicate ideas and emotions without speaking. By focusing on physical expression, actors can convey a wide range of emotions and engage the audience in a powerful and non-verbal manner.

QUESTION 126

Answer: B

Explanation: In this situation, the role of the director as an "Acting Coach" is highlighted. Acting coaches provide guidance and support to actors to help them develop their characters and enhance their performances. The director's responsibility to work closely with actors, especially those with potential but limited experience, is essential for achieving the desired artistic vision for the production.

QUESTION 127

Answer: D

Explanation: The role of the director as a "Conceptualizer" is most evident in this situation. The director is responsible for conceptualizing and shaping the overall vision and interpretation of the play. By updating certain elements while maintaining the play's authenticity, the director ensures the production resonates with modern audiences while staying true to the essence of the original script.

QUESTION 128

Answer: B

Explanation: "To Kill a Mockingbird" is a powerful and thought-provoking play that explores social issues such as racial prejudice and acceptance. The adaptation of Harper Lee's classic novel for the stage provides ample opportunities for diverse casting and fosters discussions about identity and social justice, making it an ideal choice for the theater teacher's objectives.

QUESTION 129

Answer: B

Explanation: "Waiting for Godot" by Samuel Beckett is a seminal play in the theater of the absurd genre, featuring surrealism, symbolism, and nonlinear storytelling. The play's themes of existentialism and the human condition, along with its open-ended structure, provide an excellent opportunity for experimental staging and creative interpretations by advanced theater students.

QUESTION 130

Answer: C

Explanation: While all the factors are essential, the highest priority should be given to choosing a play that aligns with the theater company's artistic vision and mission. The selected play should reflect the values and goals of the theater company, ensuring a coherent and meaningful theatrical experience for both the artists and the audience. This alignment helps create a unique and consistent identity for the theater company and fosters a loyal and engaged audience base.

QUESTION 131

Answer: D

Explanation: A theater teacher should take a careful approach when considering the age-appropriateness of a play's content. It is essential to assess the play's themes, language, and subject matter to ensure they are suitable for the intended audience, which might include students of varying age groups or the general public. The goal is to create a thought-provoking and engaging experience without exposing the audience to content that may be inappropriate or uncomfortable for them.

QUESTION 132

Answer: B

Explanation: To secure the rights to produce a copyrighted play, a theater producer must have a Memorandum of Understanding (MOU) with the playwright or the playwright's authorized representative. The MOU outlines the terms and conditions of the licensing agreement, including performance dates, royalties, and any other contractual obligations. It is a crucial legal document that protects both the playwright's intellectual property rights and the producer's right to stage the play.

QUESTION 133

Answer: B

Explanation: Limited liability protection is a legal concept that helps protect theater producers from personal financial responsibility in case of unforeseen accidents or liabilities during a production. With limited liability, the producer's personal assets are shielded from any legal claims or debts related to the production. However, it is important to note that limited liability protection does not absolve the producer from fulfilling contractual obligations or maintaining a safe working environment for the production team and performers.

QUESTION 134

Answer: D

Explanation: While all the listed qualities are valuable, the highest priority when selecting artistic staff should be given to individuals with creativity and a strong artistic vision. Theater teachers should look for artists who can bring fresh perspectives and innovative ideas to the production. Their ability to envision and communicate a compelling artistic vision is crucial in creating a unique and impactful theatrical experience.

QUESTION 135

Answer: B

Explanation: The primary purpose of holding auditions for a theatrical production is to provide actors with an opportunity to showcase their talents and skills. Auditions allow the production team to evaluate each actor's suitability for specific roles and their ability to bring the characters to life. It is a fair and transparent process that allows actors of various levels of experience to be considered for the production.

QUESTION 136

Answer: D

Explanation: In a production with a limited budget, it is crucial to prioritize essential elements that are necessary for staging the play safely and legally. This includes securing the rights to the script, obtaining required permits, and implementing proper safety measures for the cast, crew, and audience. After addressing these crucial aspects, the remaining funds can be allocated to other important production elements, ensuring a balanced and successful theatrical experience.

QUESTION 137

Answer: C

Explanation: When planning a theatrical production, it is essential to build buffer time into the schedule to accommodate unexpected delays that may arise during rehearsals or technical preparations. These delays could be due to unforeseen circumstances, such as illness, technical difficulties, or the need for additional practice. By incorporating buffer time, the production team can adapt to challenges without compromising the overall schedule and ensuring a well-prepared and polished performance.

QUESTION 138

Answer: A

Explanation: For a tragic play, the theater teacher should focus on achieving unity and coherence in the set design. The set should reflect the mood and tone of the play, creating a harmonious and integrated visual experience for the audience. Unity in design helps reinforce the emotional impact of the story, enhancing the audience's connection with the characters and the narrative.

QUESTION 139

Answer: A

Explanation: When selecting costumes for a historical theater production, it is essential to prioritize accuracy and authenticity. The costumes should be meticulously researched and designed to reflect the fashion and style of the specific historical period in which the play is set. Authentic costumes help immerse the audience in the world of the play and add credibility to the overall production.

QUESTION 140

Answer: A

Explanation: When directing a play set in the Elizabethan era of England, the theater teacher should give the most attention to ensuring the historical accuracy of the language and dialogue used by the characters. The language during this period was distinct and often poetic, with unique phrasing and vocabulary. Staying true to the linguistic conventions of the time will enhance the authenticity of the performance and transport the audience back to the Elizabethan era.

QUESTION 141

Answer: C

Explanation: To understand the essence of Ancient Greek theater, participating in a mask-making workshop would be most effective. Masks were an integral part of Greek theater, and they played a significant role in the performances. By creating masks themselves, students can gain insights into the artistic and cultural significance of masks, the use of symbolism in Greek theater, and how the masks conveyed emotions and character archetypes.

QUESTION 142

Answer: B

Explanation: Ensuring the safety of the production and the audience is paramount. If some materials used in the set construction are not fire-retardant, the theater teacher should replace them with suitable fire-resistant alternatives. This proactive approach minimizes the risk of fire-related accidents during the performance, safeguarding the well-being of everyone involved.

QUESTION 143

Answer: C

Explanation: In writing a stage play, a strong central conflict is crucial to engaging the audience and driving the plot forward. By identifying the protagonist's main objective and the obstacles they face, the student can develop a compelling storyline that keeps the audience invested in the characters' journey. A well-defined conflict provides direction and purpose to the narrative, making it easier to develop coherent and engaging storytelling.

QUESTION 144

Answer: A

Explanation: When adapting a classic novel into a stage play, it is essential to prioritize maintaining the original storyline and dialogues as much as possible. The goal is to preserve the essence and core themes of the novel in the theatrical adaptation. While some modifications may be necessary to fit the constraints of a stage production, staying true to the original material ensures that the adaptation remains faithful to the author's intent and the source material's emotional impact.

QUESTION145

Answer: B

Explanation: Improvisation exercises can be a powerful technique to help students explore the depth of their characters. By embodying their characters and engaging in improvised scenes, students can delve into their characters' emotions, motivations, and responses to different situations. This hands-on approach allows students to develop a deeper understanding of their characters and fosters the creation of more nuanced and authentic performances in their original plays.

QUESTION 146

Answer: C

Explanation: Organizing brainstorming sessions is an effective approach to spark creativity among theater students. By providing a supportive and collaborative environment, students can freely share their ideas, bounce off each other's creativity, and build upon different perspectives. This process encourages innovative thinking, helps overcome creative blocks, and allows students to discover unique and compelling story ideas for their playmaking assignments.

QUESTION 147

Answer: C

Explanation: To strengthen the communication of ideas and feelings in a script, it's important to explore the characters' inner conflicts and desires. By delving into the characters' emotional journeys, the student can develop a more profound and meaningful theme that resonates with the audience. The characters' struggles, motivations, and growth contribute to the overall emotional impact of the play, creating a deeper connection between the audience and the story.

QUESTION 148

Answer: C

Explanation: To manage the complexity of a play with multiple storylines, using a clear timeline and signposting events is an effective approach. This helps guide the audience through the different narratives and avoids confusion. By establishing a coherent structure, the audience can follow the play's progression and connect with the characters and themes more effectively.

QUESTION 149

Answer: C

Explanation: "Waiting for Godot" by Samuel Beckett is a quintessential example of absurd theater. The play features existential themes, repetitive dialogue, and a lack of traditional narrative progression, challenging conventional notions of plot and character development. The characters' actions and conversations often appear futile, highlighting the human condition of uncertainty and existential ing.

QUESTION 150

Answer: A

Explanation: A grand palace requires a sense of grandeur and proportion. Symmetry and balance in the design help create a visually pleasing and harmonious composition, conveying the desired sense of regal magnificence.

QUESTION 151

Answer: B

Explanation: During the Renaissance, theater often served as a means to propagate religious messages and moral lessons. The plays of this era were commonly used to reinforce religious values and teachings.

QUESTION 152

Answer: D

Explanation: Diction and voice are essential elements in ensuring that the audience can understand and engage with the dialogue. Clear vocal projection and enunciation contribute to effective communication on stage.

QUESTION 153

Answer: D

Explanation: In a physical theater performance, movement and gesture become primary tools for conveying emotions, actions, and narratives. They play a central role in communicating without the use of extensive dialogue.

QUESTION 154

Answer: A

Explanation: Tragedy is characterized by its focus on intense conflicts and the exploration of profound human emotions. It often features an unresolved ending that leaves the audience contemplating the consequences of the characters' actions.

QUESTION 155

Answer: D

Explanation: Commedia dell'arte is a theatrical form originating from Italy that involves improvisational performances by actors portraying stock characters with distinct personalities and traits. Physical comedy and interactions are central to this form.

QUESTION 156

Answer: C

Explanation: In the Elizabethan era, actors utilized rhetorical delivery, a technique that involved using heightened and rhythmic vocal patterns to project their voices across the open-air theaters. This allowed the actors to reach a larger audience without the aid of microphones.

QUESTION 157

Answer: C

Explanation: Kabuki theater is known for its emphasis on physical exaggeration and stylized movements to convey emotions and characters. This technique allows for the expression of complex emotions and stories in a visually striking manner.

QUESTION 158

Answer: A

Explanation: The Meisner Technique emphasizes truthful and emotional reactions by encouraging actors to connect with their own emotional experiences. This approach helps actors create authentic and spontaneous performances.

QUESTION 159

Answer: B

Explanation: Laban Movement Analysis focuses on the use of movement and body dynamics to enhance an actor's physical expression and understanding of space. It emphasizes precision, breath, and spatial awareness in ensemble work.

QUESTION 160

Answer: D

Explanation: Chekhov's writing is known for its subtextual layering, where characters' dialogue and actions often convey underlying emotions and unspoken thoughts. This technique allows for a blend of humor and introspection as audiences discern the characters' true feelings beneath the surface.

QUESTION 161

Answer: C

Explanation: Brecht's use of alienation effects aims to disrupt the audience's emotional immersion and encourage critical thinking. By preventing emotional identification, Brecht sought to prompt the audience to reflect on social and political issues portrayed in the play.

QUESTION 162

Answer: D

Explanation: Theatre of the Absurd is characterized by its use of surreal and illogical situations, disjointed dialogue, and a departure from traditional dramatic structure. These elements create an atmosphere of absurdity and challenge conventional notions of storytelling.

QUESTION 163

Answer: D

Explanation: Brecht's epic theater aimed to keep the audience intellectually engaged and critical of the events on stage. By using techniques like alienation and breaking the fourth wall, Brecht sought to prevent emotional immersion and prompt audiences to analyze social and political issues.

QUESTION 164

Answer: C

Explanation: Adapting a stage play to a different medium often involves reshaping its elements to suit the new context while preserving the core themes and messages. This allows the adaptation to resonate with the new audience while staying true to the essence of the original work.

QUESTION 165

Answer: B

Explanation: Interweaving multiple storylines and characters can add depth and complexity to a stage play. When properly connected, these subplots can enhance the thematic unity of the play and provide a richer experience for the audience.

QUESTION 166

Answer: C

Explanation: Improvisation is a technique in which actors create scenes, dialogue, and actions on the spot, without a scripted plan. It encourages creativity, spontaneity, and the development of character-driven moments.

QUESTION 167

Answer: C

Explanation: To generate rich and diverse ideas for stories, actions, characters, and dramatic environments, theater teachers can combine multiple methods of research and information gathering. This may involve conducting interviews, engaging in fieldwork, and consulting historical documents, among other sources, to enrich their creative process.

QUESTION 168

Answer: C

Explanation: The plot is the backbone of a script, as it outlines the sequence of events and actions that drive the story forward. It determines the structure of the play and how ideas and feelings are communicated to the audience.

QUESTION 169

Answer: C

Explanation: The theme of a play represents its central message or underlying idea. It provides depth and meaning to the story, shaping how ideas and feelings are communicated to the audience.

QUESTION 170

Answer: C

Explanation: Expressionism is a dramatic style that emphasizes the emotional and psychological states of characters, often through exaggerated physicality and distorted emotions. It aims to convey the inner experiences and feelings of the characters rather than presenting a realistic portrayal.

QUESTION 171

Answer: D

Explanation: A sketch is a short, self-contained theatrical piece that usually consists of unrelated scenes or vignettes. Unlike traditional plays, sketches do not follow a linear narrative and often focus on humor, satire, or social commentary.

QUESTION 172

Answer: B

Explanation: During the Renaissance, women were not permitted to act on stage, so all female roles were performed by male actors. This convention continued for centuries until women were eventually allowed to participate in theatrical performances.

QUESTION 173

Answer: D

Explanation: Stanislavski's Method, also known as the Stanislavski System or Method Acting, is a historical style of acting that focuses on emotional realism and psychological truth. Actors using this method strive to form a deep emotional connection with their characters to deliver authentic and convincing performances.

QUESTION 174

Answer: A

Explanation: The Meisner Technique, developed by Sanford Meisner, emphasizes truthful acting through physical actions and objectives. Actors use repetition exercises and active listening to discover their character's motivations and respond spontaneously to the given circumstances.

QUESTION 175

Answer: D

Explanation: Viewpoints is a contemporary acting technique that focuses on the actor's awareness and use of spatial and movement concepts on stage. By exploring these fundamental aspects, actors can create dynamic and engaging performances that make use of the physical space and interactions with other actors.

QUESTION 176

Answer: C

Explanation: Voice modulation is the practice of varying the pitch, volume, and pace of speech to convey different emotions, intentions, and character traits. This technique is essential for actors to effectively communicate with the audience and bring their characters to life.

QUESTION 177

Answer: D

Explanation: Physical warm-up exercises in actor training aim to prepare an actor's body for the physical demands of the specific role or performance they are about to undertake. It helps improve flexibility, coordination, and focus, allowing actors to fully embody their characters and deliver convincing performances.

QUESTION 178

Answer: D

Explanation: Robert Edmond Jones was a prominent theatrical designer and director known for his innovative approach to stage design and lighting. He played a crucial role in the development of the regional theater movement, which aimed to establish professional theater companies outside of New York City, making high-quality theater accessible to audiences across the country.

QUESTION 179

Answer: D

Explanation: The 20th century saw significant advancements in multimedia and projection technology, revolutionizing theatrical production. These innovations allowed for more dynamic and immersive storytelling through the use of video projections, digital effects, and interactive media, enhancing the overall theatrical experience for audiences.

QUESTION 180

Answer: D

Explanation: Amiri Baraka, formerly known as LeRoi Jones, was a prominent African-American playwright, poet, and activist. He is celebrated for his significant contributions to African-American theater, using his works to address pressing social issues, advocate for civil rights, and explore themes of racial identity and oppression in America.

QUESTION 181

Answer: A

Explanation: The pursuit of the American Dream is a recurring theme in contemporary American drama, which delves into the dreams, challenges, and failures of ordinary individuals seeking success, happiness, and a better life. It reflects the complexities and realities of the modern American experience.

QUESTION 182

Answer: C

Explanation: Absurdist plays in American drama often feature nihilistic and existential themes, ing the meaning of life, the human condition, and the absurdity of existence. These plays typically lack traditional plot structures and challenge conventional notions of logic and reason.

QUESTION 183

Answer: D

Explanation: The New Queer Cinema movement emerged in the 1990s in response to the AIDS crisis and sought to promote LGBTQ+ rights, representation, and visibility in theater and film. It contributed to the cultural and social acceptance of queer identities and stories.

QUESTION 184

Answer: C

Explanation: Traditional Japanese Noh theater is known for its use of masks to portray characters. These masks, called Noh masks, help convey the emotions and identities of the characters, and are an integral part of the Noh performance tradition.

QUESTION 185

Answer: C

Explanation: Aboriginal Australian theater often incorporates modern Western theatrical conventions while drawing inspiration from ancient oral storytelling traditions. This blend of traditional and contemporary elements reflects the ongoing cultural exchange between Indigenous and Western artistic practices.

QUESTION 186

Answer: C

Explanation: Griot performances in Africa involve storytelling, music, dance, and elaborate costumes to convey moral lessons, historical events, and cultural values. Griots, the performers and storytellers, play a significant role in preserving and transmitting the oral traditions and heritage of their communities.

QUESTION 187

Answer: C

Explanation: The "Yes, and..." rule in improvisation encourages actors to accept and build upon their scene partner's ideas, rather than denying or contradicting them. This fosters a collaborative and supportive environment, allowing the scene to progress organically and creatively.

QUESTION 188

Answer: C

Explanation: Mirroring is an improvisation technique where one actor imitates the physical actions and emotions of another actor in real-time. It requires close observation and synchronization between the actors, leading to unique and spontaneous interactions on stage.

QUESTION 189

Answer: A

Explanation: A thrust stage configuration extends into the audience, surrounding it on three sides, which creates an intimate and immersive theatrical experience. This arrangement allows the audience to be closer to the performers, fostering a stronger connection and engagement with the play's events.

QUESTION 190

Answer: B

Explanation: Blocking in theater refers to the precise positioning and movement of actors on the stage during a performance. It is a crucial aspect of staging, as it determines the physical relationships between characters, the use of the stage space, and the visual composition of the scenes.

QUESTION 191

Answer: C

Explanation: When selecting a play for a school production, it is essential to consider how well the play aligns with the school's educational objectives and values. The chosen play should offer opportunities for learning, personal growth, and align with the educational mission of the school.

QUESTION 192

Answer: D

Explanation: In selecting a play for a community theater, it is crucial to consider the diversity of characters and themes portrayed in the play. This ensures inclusivity and representation for a broad range of community members, fostering a sense of belonging and engagement within the theater community.

QUESTION 193

Answer: B

Explanation: The principle of repetition in theatrical design involves the use of similar visual elements, such as shapes, colors, or patterns, to create a sense of cohesion and unity throughout the production's design. It helps tie different elements together, creating a cohesive and visually appealing composition.

QUESTION 194

Answer: C

Explanation: The principle of emphasis in theatrical design involves creating visual focus on a specific element or area on the stage. This is achieved through the use of contrast, scale, color, or lighting, directing the audience's attention to the most significant or meaningful aspects of the production.

QUESTION 195

Answer: B

Explanation: In designing the set for a tragic play, the principles of balance and contrast can be applied by using a variety of colors and shapes to create visual interest. This helps set the emotional tone and atmosphere of the play, enhancing its impact on the audience.

QUESTION 196

Answer: B

Explanation: In costume design for an ensemble cast production, the principles of repetition and unity can be applied by repeating similar patterns and textures throughout the costumes. This creates a cohesive and unified look for the ensemble, enhancing the sense of collaboration and teamwork among the characters.

QUESTION 197

Answer: C

Explanation: Euripides, an ancient Greek playwright, is known for his tragic plays that delve into the complexities of the human condition. Many of his works, such as "Medea" and "The Bacchae," explore themes of pride, hubris, and the consequences of human actions.

QUESTION 198

Answer: B

Explanation: Molière, a French playwright, is celebrated for his farcical comedies that use humor and satire to critique social conventions and human foibles. Works like "Tartuffe" and "The Misanthrope" are prime examples of his comedic genius.

QUESTION 199

Answer: C

Explanation: American theater during the 20th century saw the rise of experimental and avant-garde theater movements that challenged traditional theatrical conventions. Playwrights and theater artists experimented with new forms, styles, and themes, pushing the boundaries of theatrical expression.

QUESTION 200

Answer: B

Explanation: The Harlem Renaissance was a cultural and artistic movement in the 1920s that celebrated and promoted African-American art, literature, and culture. In American theater, it led to a surge of African-American playwrights, actors, and works that celebrated black identity and experiences, enriching the diversity and cultural landscape of American dramatic literature.

QUESTION 201

Answer: B

Explanation: Existentialist drama often delves into the philosophical themes of the absurdity and meaninglessness of human existence. Playwrights like Samuel Beckett and Jean-Paul Sartre explored the struggles and existential dilemmas faced by individuals trying to find purpose and significance in an indifferent and chaotic world.

QUESTION 202

Answer: C

Explanation: Postmodern drama is characterized by its willingness to blend various styles, genres, and cultural references, challenging the boundaries of traditional theatrical forms. This eclecticism reflects the postmodern era's ing of fixed truths and grand narratives, inviting audiences to engage with the complexity and multiplicity of perspectives in contemporary society.

QUESTION 203

Answer: B

Explanation: As a theater director, it is essential to create a collaborative environment where ideas can be explored and discussed openly. While the actor's suggestion might be valid, it is crucial to consider the original intent of the play and its emotional impact on the audience. By involving the entire cast and crew in the discussion, you can make an informed decision that aligns with the artistic vision of the production.

QUESTION 204

Answer: D

Explanation: As a theater producer, it is essential to balance artistic aspirations with financial realities. Hiring a well-known actor can boost ticket sales and visibility, but exceeding the budget could lead to financial difficulties. Instead of compromising on artistic choices, seeking additional funding or sponsors is a proactive approach to cover the higher salary and ensure a successful production.

QUESTION 205

Answer: C

Explanation: As a designer, it is essential to find creative solutions that strike a balance between artistic vision and budget constraints. By simplifying the set design and lighting effects while retaining the core elements of the director's vision, you can still create a visually impactful production without jeopardizing financial stability.

QUESTION 206

Answer: B

Explanation: To understand Greek theater, students need to explore the original ancient Greek texts and their cultural significance. By analyzing works like "Medea" and "Oedipus Rex," students can gain insights into the themes, storytelling techniques, and societal aspects of Greek theater. This approach provides a strong foundation for comprehending the historical and artistic significance of Greek drama.

QUESTION 207

Answer: C

Explanation: Group activities and ensemble-based exercises can help shy students feel more comfortable and secure within a team. By creating a supportive and inclusive environment, the student can gradually build confidence and trust in their peers, leading to increased active involvement in class activities. Solo performances (Option A) might add unnecessary pressure, while written assignments (Option D) may not fully address the student's need for self-expression through performance.

QUESTION 208

Answer: B

Explanation: Option B provides an opportunity for students to explore the connections between visual art and theater. By visiting an art gallery and discussing how visual art influences set design, students can witness firsthand how different art forms collaborate and inspire each other in theatrical productions. This activity demonstrates the interdisciplinary nature of theater and encourages students to draw inspiration from various artistic disciplines.

QUESTION 209

Answer: C

Explanation: As a director, it is essential to support and guide your actors through the rehearsal process. One-on-one sessions provide a safe and focused environment where actors can explore their characters' motivations, emotions, and personal connections. By understanding their characters on a deeper level, the actors can deliver more authentic and impactful performances without compromising the play's authenticity.

QUESTION 210

Answer: B

Explanation: Producing a musical with high production costs carries inherent financial risks. Securing insurance is a proactive measure that can protect the production company from severe financial losses in case the show does not meet expected revenue targets. While scaling down the production (Option C) is a viable option, it might affect the artistic integrity of the musical. Insurance provides a safety net, allowing producers to take calculated risks while safeguarding the company's financial stability.

QUESTION 211

Answer: A

Explanation: Video projections can be a creative solution to overcome space limitations while still creating a sense of grandeur and historical accuracy. By using projected backgrounds, you can transport the audience to ancient Rome and provide the illusion of vast and intricate settings without physically building large set pieces. This approach allows for flexibility in design and enhances the overall visual experience of the production.

QUESTION 212

Answer: D

Explanation: Encouraging students to engage actively with Noh theater will deepen their appreciation and understanding of its unique qualities. By assigning them to adapt a famous Western play into a Noh-style performance, students must explore and apply Noh's stylistic and symbolic elements, making the experience more hands-on and immersive. This activity encourages creative thinking and allows students to draw connections between different theatrical traditions.

QUESTION 213

Answer: B

Explanation: Beginning with simple improv games that emphasize trust and cooperation helps create a safe and supportive environment for students. These games allow students to feel comfortable with each other, build confidence, and develop essential improvisational skills without the pressure of specific roles or scenarios. Gradually, as students gain confidence, more complex improv activities can be introduced.

QUESTION 214

Answer: D

Explanation: Option D provides a hands-on and immersive experience for students, allowing them to explore the intersection of theater and dance in a practical way. Through collaboration, theater students and dance students can learn from each other's artistic processes and create a unique performance that combines elements of both art forms. This activity emphasizes the interdisciplinary nature of theater and fosters a deeper appreciation for the connections between different artistic expressions.

QUESTION 215

Answer: B

Explanation: Option B allows the production to maintain its artistic integrity while finding cost-effective solutions. Creative lighting techniques can create the illusion of grandeur and atmosphere, even with minimalistic set pieces. This approach demonstrates the director's ability to think innovatively and adapt to challenges, providing the audience with a visually captivating experience without compromising the production's budget.

QUESTION 216

Answer: C

Explanation: As a director, it is essential to support and guide your actors through challenging material. Individual sessions allow struggling actors to delve deeper into their characters' emotions and motivations. By understanding the characters' emotional journeys, actors can authentically portray their roles, leading to more compelling and impactful performances. Replacing actors (Option A) or modifying the script (Option D) might compromise the artistic vision of the production.

QUESTION 217

Answer: C

Explanation: Option C promotes effective collaboration by fostering open communication and acknowledging the value of each individual's contributions. In a community theater setting, volunteers often have different levels of experience and expertise. By creating a supportive environment where everyone feels heard and respected, the team can work together harmoniously, leading to a more successful and enriching production.

QUESTION 218

Answer: C

Explanation: Option C addresses the concern by setting clear expectations and emphasizing the importance of time management for both academics and theater commitments. By providing a well-structured rehearsal schedule and encouraging students to prioritize their responsibilities, you create a conducive environment for the students to participate in the production without compromising their academics. Offering academic support (Option D) can be helpful but might not fully address the concern about time commitment.

QUESTION 219

Answer: B

Explanation: Option B promotes effective communication and collaboration between the stage manager and the lighting designer. Addressing the issue together allows for immediate adjustments to ensure the lighting cues align with the actors' movements. Taking over the lighting controls (Option A) might not be feasible or practical during a tech rehearsal, and relying solely on the director (Option C) could lead to miscommunication. Option D might divide responsibilities but may not be the most efficient approach to resolve the issue promptly.

QUESTION 220

Answer: C

Explanation: Option C is essential for the success of a theater tour. Clear and efficient communication is crucial in managing the logistics, scheduling, and coordination of performances in different cities. It ensures that the entire team is on the same page, minimizing the risk of miscommunication or missed opportunities. While maximizing seating capacity (Option A) and minimizing production costs (Option B) are relevant considerations, effective communication is a fundamental aspect of successful theater touring. Relying solely on local theater communities (Option D) might not provide the level of control and consistency needed for a smooth tour.

QUESTION 221

Answer: B

Explanation: At different age levels, it's essential to recognize developmental differences and prioritize specific aspects of performance. For middle school students, encouraging and nurturing emotional expression and physical gestures is important for their growth. While line delivery is significant, the focus should be on holistic development rather than punitive measures.

QUESTION 222

Answer: B

Explanation: Collaborative efforts between theater and related arts disciplines are crucial for a successful production. Addressing synchronization issues requires cooperation between theater and music students. Joint rehearsals will help them understand each other's cues and timing, enhancing the overall performance quality.

QUESTION 223

Answer: B

Explanation: Theater is a reflection of the cultural, social, and political contexts of its time. The opulence and grandeur of the Elizabethan era were often influenced by the values and status symbols of that society. Understanding these connections between theater and the humanities provides valuable insights into historical and artistic contexts.

QUESTION 224

Answer: C

Explanation: Natural dialogue is essential for engaging and authentic storytelling. Observing real conversations helps writers capture the nuances of human speech, making characters relatable and the story more immersive. Dialogue should mirror the way people communicate while serving the plot and character development.

QUESTION 225

Answer: B

Explanation: Understanding a character's emotions and motivations is fundamental to authentic acting. By delving into the character's psyche, the actor can connect on a deeper level and convey genuine emotions. This approach enhances the overall performance and creates a more compelling portrayal.

QUESTION 226

Answer: C

Explanation: At a young age, fostering self-expression and confidence is crucial. Evaluating based on effort and growth acknowledges the shy student's progress and encourages their development. It's essential to create a supportive environment that values each child's unique journey in theater.

QUESTION 227

Answer: C

Explanation: Different genres demand unique approaches and techniques. Evaluating performances based on their respective conventions and execution acknowledges the strengths and challenges of each style. This approach ensures a fair assessment of the students' efforts and creativity.

QUESTION 228

Answer: C

Explanation: Collaboration is key to successful interdisciplinary projects. Encouraging both groups to work together ensures a balanced and cohesive performance. This approach allows the students to leverage their respective strengths while addressing the issue of overshadowing.

QUESTION 229

Answer: C

Explanation: Theater often reflects and responds to the historical, social, and cultural context of its time. Guiding the student to explore historical connections enhances their understanding of the play's significance and deepens their critical thinking skills.

QUESTION 230

Answer: C

Explanation: Ancient Greek theater holds enduring value as it delved into fundamental aspects of the human experience. Themes such as fate, morality, and the human condition explored in Greek plays are still relevant today and have significantly influenced modern theater and literature.

QUESTION 231

Answer: C

Explanation: Theater has the power to stimulate philosophical contemplation by presenting complex situations and moral dilemmas. Through character interactions and narratives, theater can prompt audiences to reflect on ethical, existential, and societal s, making it a valuable medium for philosophical exploration.

QUESTION 232

Answer: C

Explanation: A cohesive and structured storyline is crucial for engaging and meaningful storytelling. Helping the students understand the significance of a central theme and interconnected plotlines will lead to a more focused, compelling, and satisfying play for both creators and audiences.

QUESTION 233

Answer: C

Explanation: Characters are the heart of a play, and their development contributes to the depth and resonance of the story. Well-developed characters engage the audience's empathy, making their journeys and interactions pivotal to the plot's progression and impact.

QUESTION 234

Answer: C

Explanation: Conveying conflicting emotions authentically requires understanding the character's motivations and context. Exploring how the character's experiences and situation give rise to these emotions will help the student create a layered and nuanced portrayal.

Milton Keynes UK
Ingram Content Group UK Ltd.
UKHW050848101023
430300UK00015B/137